BECOMING
EUCHARISTIC
PEOPLE

"Laying out a compelling vision for parish life, Tim O'Malley's latest work is bold, brilliant, captivating, and accessible. Thoughtful and well researched, it is balanced with inherent practicality. This is a nuanced and insightful approach to cultivating Eucharistic parish communities, and I highly recommended you read it and work through the assessment process it offers."

Julianne Stanz
Director of Discipleship and Parish Life
Diocese of Green Bay

"*Becoming Eucharistic People* is a beautiful and much-needed guide for parish renewal in and through the Eucharist. Timothy O'Malley offers a compelling path of Eucharistic revival with practical suggestions and resources for both clergy and laity. This book is perfect for small groups and ministry teams and is a must-read for all concerned about evangelization, the Eucharist, and the renewal of our parishes, families, Church, and society."

Andrew W. Lichtenwalner
Director of the Office of Formation and Discipleship
Archdiocese of Atlanta

"For every parish wringing its hands over disaffiliation, post-pandemic revitalization, and ministering in a deeply fractured Church and world—for every parish—Tim O'Malley provides an indispensable resource and words of tremendous hope. This is not another quick-fix parish renewal program; *Becoming Eucharistic People* is transformative, challenging Church leaders to set aside everything they thought they knew about building community. At the same time inspirational and practical, this book encourages a distinctly Catholic culture that is laser-focused on the Eucharist, boldly public, gritty, and real. O'Malley is a visionary, painting a picture of the parish as the hub of common life where 'every tabernacle light serves as a memorial witness' to Jesus Christ alive among us. To Church leaders at every level: Don't plan one more thing until you read this book!"

Karen Shadle
Director of the Office of Worship
Archdiocese of Louisville

Books in the Engaging Catholicism series from the McGrath Institute for Church Life at the University Notre Dame help readers discover the beauty and truth of the Catholic faith through a concise exploration of the Church's most important but often difficult-to-grasp doctrines as well as crucial pastoral and spiritual practices. Perfect for seekers and new Catholics, clergy and catechetical leaders, and everyone in between, the series expands the McGrath Institute's mission to connect the Catholic intellectual life at Notre Dame to the pastoral life of the Church and the spiritual needs of her people.

Praise for the Engaging Catholicism series:

"The Engaging Catholicism series offers clear and engaging presentations of what we Catholics believe and how we practice our faith. These books are written by experts who know how to keep things accessible yet substantive, and there is nothing fluffy or light about them. They should be in the hand of anyone who simply wants to live their faith more deeply every day and to share it with others who teach, pastor, or parent."

Katie Prejean McGrady
Catholic author, speaker, and host of the *Ave Explores* podcast

"The Engaging Catholicism series is a powerful tool to bring the beauty and depth of our Catholic theological tradition to those who need it most. This series will help many to truly engage our Catholic faith."

Most Rev. Andrew Cozzens
Auxiliary Bishop of Saint Paul and Minneapolis

ENGAGING CATHOLICISM

BECOMING
EUCHARISTIC
PEOPLE

The Hope and Promise
of Parish Life

Timothy P. O'Malley

McGrath Institute for Church Life | University of Notre Dame

AVE MARIA PRESS AVE Notre Dame, Indiana

Nihil Obstat: Reverend Monsignor Michael Heintz, PhD, *Censor Librorum*
Imprimatur: Most Reverend Kevin C. Rhoades, Bishop of Fort Wayne–South Bend
  December 8, 2021

Foreword © 2022 by Bishop Andrew H. Cozzens

Founded in 1865, Ave Maria Press is a ministry of the United States Province of Holy Cross.

www.avemariapress.com

Paperback: ISBN-13 978-1-64680-156-5

E-book: ISBN-13 978-1-64680-157-2

Special Edition product number: 30009

Cover image of "The Triumph of the Cross" is from the apse of the Basilica San Clemente, Rome.

Cover and text design by Samantha Watson.

Printed and bound in the United States of America.

Library of Congress Cataloging-in-Publication Data
Names: O'Malley, Timothy P., author.
Title: Becoming eucharistic people : the hope and promise of parish life / Timothy P. O'Malley.
Description: Notre Dame, Indiana : Ave Maria Press, [2022] | Series: Engaging Catholicism | Includes bibliographical references. | Summary: "In this book Timothy P. O'Malley probes what it means to foster a Eucharistic reverence and understanding of the real presence of Christ in a Catholic parish through reverent and joyful liturgies, formation in catechesis, solidarity with neighbor, and support of the domestic Church"-- Provided by publisher.
Identifiers: LCCN 2021062171 (print) | LCCN 2021062172 (ebook) | ISBN 9781646801565 (paperback) | ISBN 9781646801572 (ebook)
Subjects: LCSH: Christian life--Catholic authors. | Jesus Christ--Presence. | Parishes. | Lord's Supper--Real presence. | BISAC: RELIGION / Christianity / Catholic | RELIGION / Christian Rituals & Practice / Sacraments
Classification: LCC BX2350.3 .O49 2022 (print) | LCC BX2350.3 (ebook) | DDC 248.4/82--dc23/eng/20220211
LC record available at https://lccn.loc.gov/2021062171
LC ebook record available at https://lccn.loc.gov/2021062172

To my teachers,
John C. Cavadini
and
Bruce T. Morrill, SJ

CONTENTS

FOREWORD

I have a very vivid memory of a retreat I led for young people as a young priest. We had spent the day giving talks, leading the retreatants in small groups, offering them confession, and in the evening we had a time of Eucharistic Adoration. As I sat at the back of the group of about fifty high school youth kneeling and praying in adoration, the movement of the Spirit of God was palpable, I could almost see how our Eucharistic Lord was working in their hearts. I was filled with gratitude and as I was thanking the Lord, he spoke to my own heart, "This is all you have to do: bring them to me in the Eucharist and let me work." Years later I would realize this is what Pope Francis would call a culture of encounter, and I would see how central this encounter was for the work of evangelization. We provided a space for these young people to encounter the living Lord and it allowed them to open their hearts to Jesus Christ and his Church.

Decades later, I now serve as the bishop of Crookston, Minnesota and I am the bishop charged with leading the US Church in a process of Eucharistic revival. After years of service in parishes and institutions, and working with various evangelistic movements, I'm convinced that the renewal of the Church will not come through programs but through a deeper encounter with the Eucharistic Lord. I am convinced we need this, not just because studies show many Catholics don't understand the Eucharist, but because Jesus Christ in the Eucharist has the power to transform lives, if we invite people to encounter him.

All of this may seem a bit naïve. After all, the challenges facing US Catholicism are steep. Internally, there is much distrust in the Church. Many people—quite naturally—are wary of their bishops after the fall-out from the sexual abuse crisis. Disaffiliation and secularization are on the rise. Many Catholics are fighting with each other. Is the Eucharist really going to help?

Externally, the challenges are equally steep. Many people have experienced loss during the COVID-19 pandemic. We have been cut off from each other. In the summer of 2020—in the very city where I was serving as an auxiliary bishop—we experienced anew the injustice of racism with the death of George Floyd. Migrants continue to suffer at our borders. And our country continues to support abortion in ways that no other nation does. How is the Eucharist going to serve as a source of healing in this time of unrest? Can the Eucharistic revival really play a part in renewing the Church and society?

In this book, Dr. Timothy P. O'Malley from the McGrath Institute for Church Life at the University of Notre Dame provides one answer to this question: spending time before the Eucharistic Lord helps build the kind of culture that fosters a Eucharistic communion.

O'Malley suggests that this culture involves four dimensions. Reverent and enculturated Eucharistic worship, an integral Eucharistic formation that attends to all the possible sources for catechesis, an approach to Catholic life that recognizes that every dimension of our lives—both public and private—is to be understood as Eucharistic, and a cultivation of a Eucharistic solidarity that transforms the parish and neighborhood alike.

O'Malley's book is not just an argument. It's an invitation to the common task of discernment for Catholic parishes, schools, and apostolates to carefully examine whether the Eucharist is the source and summit of their lives. This book invites hard but salutary questions. Is our worship reverent? Does our catechesis attend to the whole person? Does the presence of Jesus Christ in the Eucharist lead men and women toward a more profound witness to divine love in the world?

In fact, these are the kind of questions that come about when you spend time with Jesus Christ in the Eucharist. The insights you have when you recognize that the Eucharist is a sacrifice of love, calling the whole Church to a deeper self-gift and deeper communion.

O'Malley, in the end, doesn't provide a program. He provides a blueprint for a Eucharistic revival that has the power to heal the wounds of Church and society alike. Such a revival, in the end, is not a program, but an awakening awareness that the meaning of the world is love: God's love. Given, poured out, and shared. It is this love that changes everything.

The Most Reverend Andrew H. Cozzens
Bishop of Crookston, Minnesota

SERIES FOREWORD

Doctrine is probably not the first thing that comes to mind when we consider the pastoral work of the Church. We tend to presume that doctrine is abstract, of interest primarily to theologians and clergy whose vocation it is to contemplate lofty questions of belief. On the other hand, we tend to think the pastoral life of the Church is consumed primarily with practical questions: How do we pray? How do we pass on faith to the next generation? How do we form Christians to care about the hungry and thirsty? How might our parishes become spaces of lived discipleship? What are the best practices for the formation of Catholic families? Presenting at catechetical conferences in dioceses on a specific point of Catholic theology, faculty and staff of the McGrath Institute for Church Life often hear the question, "So, what's the significance? Give me the practical takeaways."

The separation between doctrine and practice is bad for theologians, pastoral leaders, and Christians looking to grow in holiness. It leads to theologians who no longer see their vocation as connected to the Church. Academic theologians speak a language that the enlightened alone possess. On occasion, they turn their attention to the ordinary beliefs and practices of the faithful, sometimes reacting with amusement or horror that one could be so primitive as to adore the Eucharist or leave flowers before Our Lady of Guadalupe. The proper arena for the theologian to exercise her craft is assumed to be the doctoral seminar, not the parish or the Catholic secondary school.

Likewise, pastoral strategy too often develops apart from the intellectual treasury of the Church. Such strategy is unreflective, not able to critically examine its own assumptions. For example, how we prepare adolescents for Confirmation is a theological and pastoral problem. Without the wisdom of sacramental doctrine, responding to this pastoral need becomes a matter of pragmatic conjecture, unfortunately leading to the variety of both implicit and often impoverished theologies of Confirmation that arose in the twentieth century. Pastoral strategy divorced from the doctrinal richness of the Church can leave catechesis deprived of anything worthwhile to pass on. If one is to be a youth minister, it is not enough to know best practices for accompanying teens through adolescence, since one can accompany someone even off a cliff. Pastoral leaders must also know a good deal about what Catholicism teaches to lead members of Christ's Body to the fullness of human happiness.

The Engaging Catholicism series invites you to see the intrinsic and intimate connection between doctrine and the pastoral life of the Church. Doctrines, after all, are the normative way of handing on the mysteries of our faith. Doctrines make us able to pick up a mystery, carry it around, and hand it to someone else. Doctrines, studied and understood, allow us to know we *are* handing on *this* mystery and not some substitute.

In order to properly hand on the mysteries of our faith, the pastoral leader has to *know a given doctrine contains a mystery*—has to have the doctrine opened up so that receiving it means encountering the mystery it carries. Only then can one be transformed by the doctrine. The problem with religious practice unformed or inadequately formed by doctrine is that it expects an easy and mostly continuous spiritual high, which cannot be sustained if one has sufficient grasp of one's own humanity. We in the McGrath Institute for Church Life have confidence in Christian doctrines as saving truths, bearing mystery from the God who is love. We believe in the importance of these teachings for making us ever more human, and we believe in the urgent need to speak the Church's doctrines into, for, and with those who tend the pastoral life of the Church. We cannot think of any task more important than this. The books of this series represent our best efforts toward this crucial effort.

John C. Cavadini
Director of the McGrath Institute for Church Life
University of Notre Dame

PREFACE

In the history of the Catholic Church, pandemics often precipitate renewal. New saints and religious orders come about. Vocations to the priesthood increase, and there is a flourishing of liturgical practice. Lay associations are formed for the renewal of post pandemic social life. This flowering of religious activity as a response to plague tends to become the occasion for a revived evangelization of societies and cultures.[1]

And yet, the Catholic Church in the United States in the late summer of 2021, as I write this, is not quite the same as Europe during the centuries of plague or as America during the Spanish Flu of 1918. The Pew and Gallup polls persistently remind us of declining religious practice among US residents.[2] The great fear post-COVID-19 is that, after months away, Catholics whose affiliation with the Church was rather thin to begin with will never come back. They did not miss the poor preaching, bad music, and a community that never knew their name. Sunday mornings can be better spent doing almost anything else, or perhaps watching part of a live-streamed Mass if it fits into the schedule.

The pandemic further revealed spaces of significant social distress in the United States. This distress has been exacerbated through social-media platforms where one can see the polarization of US citizens around racism, the wearing of masks, vaccinations, the temporary closing of churches, and anything related to politics. The violence does not stay on social media. In the United States in the summers of 2020 and 2021, gun violence increased on our city streets. Mass shootings are now a terrifying almost-monthly ritual. Too often, we see images or hear stories of young men and women of color murdered in the streets because of the color of their skin. All the while, various media outlets dial up the fear, covering such moments as spectacles for all of us to behold. In this context, our solidarity with the victim becomes a matter of partisan politics, an *anticommunion* where people are choosing sides instead of listening to the lamentations of the victim and their families who cry for justice.

This violence spills over into our parishes where baptized sons and daughters of God develop a distrust of their bishops, their priests, and one another. We see a fracturing of communion in the Church herself. At the start of the pandemic parishioners often criticized their pastors for even the most basic precautions enacted against COVID-19. They left parishes that were considered too subservient to the recommendations of the Centers for Disease Control and Prevention. Now that vaccinations are present in the United States, some Catholics are wary of any Catholic who takes a mask off. They presume that their fellow member of Christ's Body cares nothing about the common good. Some Catholics, no matter what their bishop says or does, respond with suspicion.

Local distrust, though, is only one dimension of the epidemic of suspicion in the Church. In June 2021, the US bishops met to discuss writing a teaching document on the Eucharist. The purpose of this teaching document was to foster a Eucharistic revival in the United States. Through the real presence of Jesus Christ in the Blessed Sacrament and our eating and drinking of his Body and Blood, can we relearn the art of both presence and communion in a fractured Church and world?

The extent of this fractured communion emerged in the bishops' own discussion of this Eucharistic document and the subsequent revival. Despite the theological expansiveness of the proposed text, most of the focus was around a section on Eucharistic coherence and political life. At least for a term (2020–2024), the United States has a Catholic President for the second time. President Joe Biden is an active Mass-goer, a Catholic in the public sphere, who also holds a variety of positions that contradict Church teaching, including on abortion, religious liberty, and gay marriage. Some bishops have called for President Biden to be denied Communion at Mass because of these positions.

At times, the debate over the document took up some of the very same partisan back-and-forth that too often defines politics in our age. In the intervening months, despite the many bishops that told Church and world alike that the document was about the Eucharist and not President Biden, few believed it. People began to take sides. We don't need a document on the Eucharist, some argued. What we really need is ecclesial reform. Rather than wait for the document to be released, everyone seemed to have made up their minds about what was in the text. In the days leading up to the bishop's November 2021 meeting, many blogs said that the bishops were meeting in Baltimore to determine whether or not to excommunicate President Biden. A copy of the document was released before the meeting, and at once there were negative reactions, especially on Twitter. Why do the bishops care so much about real presence and not about social injustice? Why are the bishops wasting money on a national Eucharistic Congress in 2024 when they could be helping the hungry and thirsty? Is this really a way for the US bishops to stick it to Pope Francis?

When the US bishops gathered in Baltimore, it became clear that much of the drama around the teaching document (entitled "The Mystery of the Eucharist in the Life of the Church") was manufactured.[3] The document, despite the claim of detractors, is a faithful representation of the Second Vatican Council's Eucharistic vision of the Church. It is attuned to the totality of Pope Francis' own magisterial teaching. The opening paragraph begins with Pope Francis' presiding over the rite of Eucharistic Exposition and Benediction during the COVID-19 pandemic. From there, the text re-proposes to the Church a vision for ecclesial renewal grounded in Eucharistic sacrifice, real presence, and the communion of self-giving love that makes up the very identity of the Church. The Church makes the Eucharist, and yet more fundamentally, it is the Eucharist that constitutes the Church.

Affiliated with this document is the proposal for a three-year Eucharistic Revival in our parishes, schools, families, and neighborhoods. This Eucharistic Revival seeks to renew the local Church through greater appreciation of the Eucharistic mystery, of the sacrificial presence of Jesus Christ that is the very reason for the Church's existence in the first place. At the end of this three-year process, there will be a national Eucharistic Congress in Indianapolis. This national gathering is only one part of the Revival. The heart of it is local renewal—a recommitment of every parish, school, and family to become what is received in the Eucharist, a communion of love poured out for the life of the world.

Both the document and Eucharistic Revival are integral to the Church's renewal in the post-COVID era. Yes, the pandemic has led to the death of tens of thousands of Americans, the cancellation of rites of passage, and too often taught us to view our neighbor as a source of contagion rather than a human being to be loved. Yes, we are more polarized as both Church and world than we have ever been before. We fight over everything on social media, distrusting all figures of authority. Yes, the Church is losing parishioners to the complex dynamics of disaffiliation. But in the midst of such crises, we are not to lose hope. It is through a Eucharistic renewal that we can remember anew what it means to belong to the People of God, the Body of Christ, and the Temple of the Holy Spirit. We are not a bureaucracy or an NGO but a communion of men and women called to the supper of the Lamb.

It is the contention of this book that the Eucharist can provide every parish in the United States with a renewed mission for evangelization that is centered around the presence of Jesus Christ, and yet calls us to the margins to foster a communion of love that can transform every crack and crevice of the cosmos. On the night before Jesus Christ died, in which he handed himself over to the darkness of the human heart, he took bread and wine and gave it to his disciples. At the precise moment in which our Lord knew the sordid depths of anticommunion, he responded through self-giving love. He gave over the very Body that men and women would inflict violence upon. Through speaking a word of love, a word that he backed up through the gift of himself for the life of the world, he reestablished communion between God and the entire human family. Even now, in every parish church throughout this world, this sacrifice of love is celebrated. He continues to give himself to us. Every tabernacle light serves as a memorial witness to the presence of Jesus Christ, who accompanies us in the turbulent moments of our personal lives and our social histories.

And yet, just telling people about the Eucharist is not sufficient. The crisis in the Church and world right now is not only intellectual. It is a crisis of the heart, a forgetting of the desire for total communion that is the destiny of every man and woman. This is the implicit argument of my book *Real Presence: What Does It Mean and Why Does It Matter?* (Ave Maria Press, 2021). One can make an intellectual assent to the Church's teaching around the Eucharist, understanding what is meant by real presence and transubstantiation alike. But this act of communication does not mean that an individual Catholic or even a whole parish thereby suddenly lives Eucharistically. As I wrote in that book, "We need to appropriate the doctrine, hold it in our religious imaginations, and bow down before the Blessed Sacrament before we make a real assent to real presence."[4] We must cultivate a Eucharistic culture in the parish where not only is Christ's real presence treated as a very important Catholic doctrine but his true presence in the Blessed Sacrament infuses the worldview and practices of that parish. The parish appropriates this doctrine to become a space of gift in which every man and woman is led to deeper communion with God and one another.

The task of this present book, a sequel to *Real Presence,* is to initiate a Eucharistic revival for the Church in which the presence of Jesus Christ in Word and sacrament begins to heal the malaises that we suffer from in this second decade of the twenty-first century. The problem of disaffiliation is quite real, and it is my contention that a Eucharistic culture within our parishes is integral to inviting people either back to parish life or to become Catholic in the first place.

Yes, we can invite people back to Mass. We can make commercials that woo Catholics to come home. We can have dialogue with those on the margins, listening to their cares and concerns. But what are Catholics finding when they come home, when they are convinced to give Mass a second chance? If we are polarized, unhospitable, inattentive to the margins, and perhaps treat religion as an entirely private affair, why will they stay? Or, if we celebrate the Eucharist in the most irreverent way, trying to be as efficient as possible to get people in and out so that they do not complain about disrupting their Sunday plans, should we be surprised if people think that the Blessed Sacrament is not all that important to their lives?

Despite the contentious wars that break out around the liturgy, this book asserts that it is the Eucharistic presence of Jesus Christ that can respond to polarization—the anticommunion— endemic in Church and society at present. After all, the Eucharist is never just a private encounter of an individual with our Lord. The end of the Eucharist is a foretaste of the communion of God and the human person, a communion that is to extend to our neighbors. The present distrust within the Church is evidence of an absence of Eucharistic culture defined by a common life in which we really believe that the God-man dwells among us. Through the dwelling of Christ's Body and Blood among us, we are to share a life in common infused with his Eucharistic presence. This is my body—the Body of the whole Christ, head and members—given for the world. This is my blood—the Blood of the whole Christ, head and members—given for our neighbor.

Hopefully reading this book is an occasion for a parish to reflect on each facet of what constitutes their distinctive Eucharistic culture. It is a book intended to elicit a conversion, a period of mutual discernment on the part of every member of the parish. The first chapter of the book treats anew the terms *Eucharist* and *culture*. The Eucharist, as Pope Benedict XVI teaches in *Sacramentum Caritatis (The Sacrament of Charity)*, is a mystery to be believed, celebrated, and lived. The mystery of the Eucharist is living, which means that every dimension of human life should find a place within it. And that includes the very culture of the parish. *Culture* is not just a term we use for high art (e.g., I love Renaissance culture) or ethnic communities (e.g., I love Mexican culture). Rather, it is both the implicit and explicit worldview and practices of a parish.

The title of the book, perhaps surprisingly, does not mention the word *culture*. This is because a culture is not intended only for its own sake. Culture creates a people. A Eucharistic culture will cultivate a Eucharistic people. This is what the Second Vatican Council meant by calling the Church the "People of God," those who are convoked by the sacrifice of Jesus Christ, a festive gathering of men and women whose vocation is Eucharistic through and through. As the theologian Fr. Louis Bouyer writes:

> The Church is made and unceasingly maintained through the Mass, for the Mass is the assembly in which the evangelical Word is proclaimed, the Christian faith confessed, the Bread broken, the Cup shared . . . where the Parousia is therefore hoped for. . . . This is to say that the Mass is, and is only, the Church in act, the Church becoming, sustaining, developing herself without ceasing.[5]

This does not mean that the only thing that the Church does is celebrate Mass. But it does mean that the deepest identity of every parish must be the Eucharist, the self-giving love of Jesus Christ given for the life of the world. The title of the book reflects this hope that the parish can become in the Eucharistic liturgy what she receives on the altar—and so be formed into a Eucharistic people dedicated to praise, adoration, and self-giving love unto the end. Such a Eucharistic culture is not brought about simply through following best practices to transform the parish in a year's time. It takes time to become a Eucharistic people.

The long-sighted process of transformation is the reason that a mosaic from the church of San Clemente in Rome was chosen for the cover of this book. San Clemente is an old church, consisting of multiple layers. At the lowest level of the church is a first century home and street where Christians gathered to celebrate the Eucharist. The present sanctuary is partially from the

1100s but was also transformed during the Renaissance in Rome in the seventeenth century. The mosaic from the 1100s consists of an image of Christ upon the cross, surrounded by Mary and the apostle John. Countless flowers bloom on the vine around Christ, an image of the fruitfulness of the Church born from the side of Christ. A Eucharistic culture is "cultivated" not immediately but throughout the centuries, as the presence of our Lord penetrates every crack and crevice of the cosmos, as Eucharistic worship forms a people.

The remainder of the book (chapters 2, 3, 4, and 5) presents four dimensions of a Eucharistic culture that will cultivate a parish as a Eucharistic people.[6] The book argues that a Eucharistic culture must include these four elements:

1. ***A sense of enculturated reverence*** for the celebration of the Mass and the Blessed Sacrament. We are not talking about what is often popularly called the Latin Mass but a sensibility that the Blessed Sacrament is *really* the gift of divine love that we receive and worship together in the context of the whole Eucharistic liturgy.

2. ***An integral formation that does not reduce Eucharistic catechesis to explanation of doctrine exclusively*** but attends to the memory, imagination, understanding, desire and will, and our very identity as a Eucharistic community. Such a Eucharistic catechesis will privilege the formation of the adult as an agent of cultural renewal in parish life.

3. ***A transition from a privatized approach*** to Eucharistic celebration to a public or popular Catholicism that properly

attends to work, festivity, and family in the act of Eucharistic worship.

4. ***The promotion of a Eucharistic solidarity*** in the parish in which the communion of love that is given by Jesus is explicitly shared with the world, bringing us into deeper unity with Catholics and non-Catholics alike in the neighborhood. Ultimately, it is this Eucharistic solidarity that is evidence of what the bishops are calling Eucharistic coherence.

In addition to this book, the Notre Dame Center for Liturgy—part of the McGrath Institute for Church Life at the University of Notre Dame—is creating a series of resources affiliated with this book, which will be available online at our website (http://mcgrath.nd.edu/eucharisticpeople). These include ideas for parish retreats reflecting on each dimension of Eucharistic culture, teaching resources, and videos. These resources testify to the pedagogy of the book. *Becoming Eucharistic People* is not meant exclusively for private edification but is for a common process of discernment undertaken by leaders within the parish over the course of at least two years. If there is to be a Eucharistic renewal, one that invites people to the banquet of the Lamb and heals us of the violence of enmity, we will need to become intentional Eucharistic communities. Such a transformation takes time.

Many insights in this book are the fruit of dialogue with colleagues. I am especially grateful to two colleagues. Katherine Angulo Valenzuela is the director of the McGrath Institute's Thriving in Ministry program. She asked me to address twelve lay leaders in the Church on the topic of this book. Before then, we had a series of important conversations that helped shape the direction of the project. Katherine is one of the most astute pastoral leaders in the Church today. She has a vision of how the enculturated beauty of Catholicism might enliven us with joy, and she has a heart for the margins, for those who are forgotten. I hope that I have learned just a bit of this *misericordia* (the mercy of the heart, in Latin) from her.

In addition, I want to express my gratitude to Julianne Stanz, director of the Parish Life & Evangelization Mission Team in the Diocese of Green Bay. I have known Julianne for years, but she graciously gave me time to talk through this book proposal. Many of the insights about culture, the liturgical wars plaguing dioceses, and the need for concrete resources to accompany parishes through this book were the fruit of conversations with Julianne. In the Church today, she is one of the most creative and faithful makers of culture.

I dedicate this book to two people, who have been influential for the way that I approach the Eucharistic mystery as leading to deeper affiliation and healing the malaise of polarization endemic in Church and society. First, to Prof. John C. Cavadini, my first theology teacher and now my mentor and boss at the McGrath Institute for Church Life. It was through a reading of Augustine's *City of God* as a junior in college in his class that I came to recognize what a Eucharistic culture and history could look like. John has taught more about how to avoid polarization in the Church than anyone else, as well as about the importance of devotion to the task of theology, of service to the concrete flesh-and-blood Church, and why the doctrines associated with real presence really do matter. He was the first person I met who united love of the Eucharist and love of the flesh-and-blood poor; he made it possible for me to adore the Blessed Sacrament and be inspired by the vision of Dorothy Day. I remain grateful to him as my teacher, mentor, and (for the last ten years) colleague.

Second, I dedicate this book to Fr. Bruce T. Morrill, SJ. Bruce taught me that the Eucharistic mystery demands a remembering of the victims, of those on the margins of our social life. This remembering can never become an abstraction but necessitates communion with the forgotten. Bruce is a devoted priest and scholar, a mentor who worked with graduate students to read the most complex of texts. He did not seek to replicate himself (rare in the academy), but to let more conservative and progressive students alike flourish under his tutelage. It was Bruce's witness of celebrating the Mass in remote communities in Alaska and his consistent ministry to prisoners that capture much of what I mean by Eucharistic solidarity. He continues to provide mentorship to me, extending the solidarity he offered to me as a graduate student at Boston College into my midcareer.

Anything in this book that facilitates a deeper communion with the Lord and thereby our neighbor is a testimony to these two mentors. Anything that does harm to our ecclesial Body is my own fault, my own fault, my most grievous fault. For that, I ask the forgiveness and patience of the reader. And a gift of the Eucharistic communion that we share is that if you can discern a better way to think about something, a better way to move forward, then this will only enrich my sense of Eucharistic gratitude. I look forward to hearing about what you have learned—perhaps one day even traveling to your parish to savor the fruits of your

Eucharistic culture. For it is in *your* parish that a Eucharistic revival will commence.

1.

WHAT IS EUCHARISTIC CULTURE?

Few of us think about it, but the parishes we belong to possess cultures. Here I do not exclusively mean that a parish is made up of African American, Hispanic, or German Catholics. This diversity is part of the culture of a parish, but it is not the only dimension. Culture is a worldview that includes a way of looking at reality and practicing what it means to be a Catholic. Culture forms us into a people.

We may likely presume that every parish possesses a Eucharistic culture. After all, what is the source and summit of a Catholic's life? It is the Eucharist, the memorial of Christ's Passion, Death, and Resurrection that we celebrate in our parish churches every day of the week. A good deal of our parish's life is dedicated to the celebration of the Eucharist.

And yet, a parish culture is more complex, perhaps at times even deviating from the Eucharistic vision offered by Catholicism. Our parishes in the United States exist within a wide array of cultures that may not be hospitable to a Catholic worldview. For example, many residents of the United States think about worship as a private affair. The individual chooses some of her free time on Sundays to belong to a congregation. Otherwise, this worship has nothing to do with the rest of her life.[1] We can be Catholic on Sundays, but the rest of the week, we might exercise our identities as nuclear engineers, factory workers, scientists, short-order cooks, teachers, and moms and dads. The parish may take on this private culture, never asking that the parishioners integrate faith and life. Parishioners may run off as individual family units to brunch after Mass, rarely getting to know their neighbors in the next pew. After all, in this case, the real purpose of Mass is one's individual (or nuclear family's) sanctification, not belonging to the communion of the Body of Christ with all believers.

I have belonged to parishes that thought about the Mass in this way, as a private act of devotion disconnected from the rest of our lives. Growing up, I attended a parish that had a chapel dedicated to perpetual Eucharistic Adoration. We loved the Eucharist. And yet, this parish once included an announcement in the bulletin that cruelly insulted parishioners who depended on food stamps for their livelihood. No one in the parish recognized the incongruence of perpetual Eucharistic Adoration and marginalizing the hungry and thirsty in our parish.

For Catholics, our common worship in the Eucharistic liturgy is not a private affair. It is a public act whereby the whole Body of Christ is transformed by the Eucharistic offering into a sacrifice of love for the life of the world. What we do on the altar on Sunday is a global reality, inviting the Catholic to let their flesh-and-blood bodies become living or reasonable sacrifices, "holy and pleasing to God, your spiritual worship" (Rom 12:1). There is no such thing as a private Catholic. Every Catholic is a public person, whose life witnesses to the Eucharistic presence of our Lord in the world.

A Eucharistic culture will not, therefore, be generated automatically in a parish that focuses on individual devotion. This Eucharistic culture requires occasions of common discernment. Do we offer to our parishioners a Eucharistic culture that integrates faith and life, or do we propose a privatized faith in our Sunday worship? If the latter, then we require a conversion or renewal of that culture.

WHAT IS CULTURE?

As I noted in the preface to this book, there are a variety of ways to define what we mean by *culture*. Culture could refer to nothing more than high art. We feel "cultured" when we listen to a symphony by Mozart or have spent time contemplating the art of Picasso. While art is important to human life, this approach to culture is too thin for a Eucharistic renewal of parish life. It risks confusing Catholicism for the religion of the aesthete who delights in pretty things instead of the religion centered on the sacrifice of the God-man, Jesus Christ.

Likewise, we can think about culture exclusively as an ethnic identity. Catholicism, in this case, consists of a variety of cultures. In our parishes, there are Mexican, Vietnamese, and Filipino Catholics. The goal of the parish is to include all ethnic identities. We want to feature their practices, welcoming them into the community of the Church.

The problem with this approach is that it presumes that only nonwhite ethnic identities possess a culture. Yes, Mexican, Vietnamese, and Filipino Catholics have culture(s) that may be different from the suburban Catholicism practiced at Our Lady of the Lake Catholic parish. But it is not true that Our Lady of the Lake is absent a culture. In fact, the possible difficulty that many parishioners at Our Lady of the Lake have in welcoming their fellow Catholics from Mexico is precisely because of the culture(s) of Our Lady of the Lake. To ignore the way that Our Lady of the Lake has enculturated Catholicism, often in a way that makes it difficult for anyone else to worship there except the residents of that suburban community, is a mode of bias. The parish community presumes that "we" possess a pure, unadulterated version of Catholicism, whereas the immigrants from Mexico are the cultured ones. The Mexican Catholics are exotic, whereas we are in the mainstream. We make some room for the practices of the Mexican Catholics, but in the way that a tourist on a cruise ship visits a local village. Yes, it is nice to see Our Lady of Guadalupe in our church once a year. But the rest of the year, she can return to her side chapel because our sanctuary does not have room for her. You can see the problems with such an approach, how this kind of bias would be detrimental to welcoming our Mexican brothers and sisters into our parish.

Lastly, we can think about culture exclusively as something negative. In evangelization literature, we hear "cultural Catholics" spoken about in less than flattering ways. The cultural Catholic does not fervently believe or practice Catholicism, showing up just for high holy days (Easter/Christmas) and other rites of passage. To persuade the cultural Catholic to become a "real" Catholic is often the goal of evangelization programs.

This negative sense of culture is also frequently employed in homilies. The priest speaks about the harmful dimensions of culture and society: "We live in a culture of death. A culture that does not support the family. A culture where Christianity is rendered a hostile proposition against the liberalism of modern life."

It is true that what we mean by a cultural Catholic is insufficient to the Gospel. Likewise, contemporary culture is indeed often driven by a lack of solidarity, what Pope Francis refers to as a throwaway culture, where the unborn, the elderly, the migrant, and the prisoner are considered expendable. US political culture is not always friendly to those who want to practice their faith. And yes, we have to admit that secularization is a pressure upon US Catholics today. Such realism is necessary.

But the word *culture* can also be used in a positive sense. At the Second Vatican Council, the Church defined *culture* as indicating:

> everything whereby man develops and perfects his many bodily and spiritual qualities; he strives by his knowledge and his labor, to bring the world itself under his control. He renders social life more human both in the family and the civic community, through improvement of customs and institutions. Throughout the course of time he expresses, communicates, and conserves in his works great spiritual experiences and desires, that they might be of advantage to the progress of many, even the whole human family.[2]

In this positive sense, there is no such thing as a non-cultural Catholic. Every Catholic is cultural insofar as she is a human being who lives her Catholic faith in the context of civilization. As human beings, we pass on wisdom from generation to generation through doctrines and practices that we "hand on" (the literal meaning of the word *tradition*) to the young.

The O'Malley family, for example, possesses a culture related to Notre Dame football. We order our Saturdays in the fall to the Fighting Irish by wearing certain clothes, talking about games past and present (incessantly, if you ask my spouse), going tailgating, and listening to the fight songs of Notre Dame. Without this culture, there would be no way for us to invite our children to become fans of the Fighting Irish. There would be no way for us to be the O'Malleys.

This richer sense of culture is the one that this book will adopt in thinking through the Eucharistic culture of a parish. In his study *Clashing Symbols: An Introduction to Faith and Culture*, the Jesuit priest and theologian Michael Paul Gallagher describes twelve features of this richer sense of culture that will be relevant to our consideration of the parish.[3] In the second part of this chapter, I will adapt these twelve dimensions to four principles in conversation with Pope Benedict's document on the Eucharist, *Sacramentum Caritatis (The Sacrament of Charity)*.

MICHAEL PAUL GALLAGHER'S TWELVE FEATURES OF CULTURE

1. Culture is a human creation.

This is important. Culture is not received as part of divine revelation. Because of the freedom that we possess as human beings to shape our common lives, we can change the culture of Our Lady of the Lake in such a way that conforms more truly to the Gospel. If we are inhospitable to our neighbors or live a privatized Catholicism, we can do something about it. Because of the power of the Spirit given to each of us, we can become agents of cultural renewal.

2. Culture is handed on to us and yet is interpreted differently in certain times and areas of the world.

Growing up in East Tennessee, attending a small parish in the foothills of the Great Smoky Mountain National Park, I learned to be Catholic in this context. Sure, all the rudiments of Catholic culture were passed on to me. I regularly attended Sunday Mass. I abstained from meat on Fridays during Lent and attended Stations of the Cross on Fridays. But my Catholicism took on a specific shape. I heard stories of the early Catholics in Blount County, Tennessee, worshipping out of a house church. I was regularly reminded that we were but 2 percent of the population of the entire diocese. The way that we lived our Catholic life— with the warmth of an evangelical but with the fervor of someone whose religion was often marginalized by our neighbors—was

integral to the culture of those practicing in the Diocese of Knoxville. We loved Benediction of the Blessed Sacrament, the Rosary,
and many traditional Catholic practices precisely because it made
us different from our neighbors (and not because we were reject-
ing the Second Vatican Council, which we barely thought about).
Although we shared Catholicism in common with parishioners in
the Archdiocese of Boston, even a non-Catholic would recognize
the differences between a Catholic parish in Boston and one in
Knoxville.

3. Culture often shapes our assumptions about the world in an unconscious manner.

Living in Boston from 2006 to 2010, I picked up certain ways
of viewing the world that were rather different from those in
my eventual home in South Bend, Indiana. When I went to the
grocery store in South Bend, I did not expect the clerk to ask me
what I was doing for the weekend. In fact, because of my time
in Boston, I viewed this as a rude intrusion upon my privacy. I
was not right to see my fellow human being with such suspicion.
Still, after living in the culture of New England, I had come to
see such questions as a form of intimacy inappropriate to share
with a stranger. I did not adopt this viewpoint consciously but
picked it up in the water (along with rooting for the Patriots and
the Red Sox).

4. Culture proposes a whole way of life that gives me an identity within a community of other persons.

The Notre Dame experience—often referred to among my undergraduate students—is a comprehensive proposal related to the identity of the students. It means being able to talk about what dorm you live in, thinking about the act of education in a particular way, tailgating and going to football games, choosing which of the two dining halls on campus is superior, commiserating about South Bend winters, and going to this or that local watering hole (after you turn twenty-one, of course). This comprehensive culture allows students at Notre Dame to share solidarity across classes. A Notre Dame graduate from 1975 shares a worldview, stories, and practices in common with a Notre Dame graduate from 2025.

5. Culture consists of both stuff and a way of interpreting the world.

Catholicism, for example, is a sacramental culture. We worship using matter. You likely know that you have found a Catholic when she is wearing a scapular, she fasts on Good Friday, she crosses herself when entering a church, and she genuflects before entering her pew. These are some of the visible and tangible things of Catholicism. Taken together, this stuff forms us to see the world differently, to engage in a process of interpretation that is not reducible only to the tangible. We view creation as revelatory of God. We have a positive view of the body. We recognize the places where God is revealing himself in the world today. The use of sacramentals in worship, where the whole created order is employed in liturgy, shapes a sacramental imagination for Catholics that makes it possible for us to see creation as revealing the mystery of divine love.

6. Culture must be comprehended in terms of meanings or beliefs, values, and customs or practices.

If you go to New Orleans during Mardi Gras, there are certain meanings and beliefs that are proposed about what it means to be human. Human beings are made not just for work but also for festivity. Carnival turns the world upside down much as the Gospel does. There are ways of behavior that are proposed, values that might otherwise seem out of place. If I showed up wearing plastic beads or carrying a coconut and a to-go cup of the finest daiquiri this side of paradise in the city of Cleveland, there would be inevitable confusion (and a possible arrest). In New Orleans, during Mardi Gras—and who am I kidding, the rest of the year—there are norms proposed about human behavior that are unique to that city. And these norms are passed on through the cycle of feasts and seasons related to Mardi Gras. You get a King Cake starting at Epiphany. You find the baby in the King Cake, making you the king or queen of the party and tasked with bringing the next King Cake to the next party. You start going to parades three weeks before the start of Lent. Meanings, morals, and tradition make up the culture of Mardi Gras in New Orleans.

7. Culture is closely linked to both institutions and symbols.

In Catholicism, one can see this in the very person and office of the pope. Integral to Catholic culture is unity. We profess belief in one, holy, Catholic, and apostolic Church. The pope is the institutional manifestation and symbol of this unity, of a Church that seeks to bring all human beings into an encounter with Christ. Through union and love of the pope—in his role, not because we love his personality—Catholics experience union with one another. The arms of St. Peter's Square open to the city of Rome and to the whole world. This art and architecture of the Vatican itself is a symbol of the vocation of the pope, who although residing in Rome seeks to promote unity with the rest of the world.

8. Culture is related to basic human practices, which are often full of meaning.

Fr. Gallagher gives the example of eating. The need to eat is shared by all human beings. And yet, eating comes to take on different meanings through the practices that we engage in while consuming food. At a wedding banquet, people must eat, but there is more to a wedding banquet than nutrition. There may be toasts feting the bride and the groom, first dances, and cutting a special cake. It is through the mundane act of eating that the very meaning of marriage is expressed within a culture. This is an august moment, a rite of passage, in which the couple passes into a new state of life. We, the community of their friends and family, surround them during this rite of passage.

9. Culture always includes a religious dimension.

Because culture has something to do with ultimate meanings, then it must eventually deal with the transcendent, proposing a "god" to be worshipped. For this reason, secularization and disaffiliation in the Church is not really a matter of atheism. Take those who find their ultimate fulfillment in the cultural world of politics. The election of the leader, the almost messianic prophet who comes to unite the nation, becomes the "god." There are shirts, hats, and rituals that come to be associated with this politician. If the politician loses, then there is almost a palpable sense that one's "god" has died. But the political cycle eventually chooses a new god for us to worship, the advent of a new politician who will bring the unity that we desire. Even the most secular person, who participates in political culture in this manner, cannot escape worshipping someone or something.

10. Culture seeks to communicate itself.

Because culture seeks to communicate itself, education into a culture is often tacit or implicit rather than explicit or stated. Catholics in the 1950s did not spend much time thinking about what it meant to pass on Catholic faith to future generations. It naturally meant participating in parish festivals, receiving catechesis, going to Mass, and worshipping in the home. But when there is a time of transition—such as our own age—culture may not communicate itself as easily. There are fewer parish festivals, and going to Mass (or honoring the Sabbath at all) is no longer considered necessary to be a good American. Because of these changes, we likely need to be more intentional about cultivating a culture, more intentional about communicating to fellow Catholics why certain practices matter to us.

11. Culture requires constant discernment, being attentive to the ways that it harms, rather than contributes to, human flourishing.

We have addressed the culture of Mardi Gras in New Orleans. Carnival is a turning upside down, a moment in which the norms of social life are temporality reversed during a festive season. But some of those reversals of norms are not healthy. The flourishing of men and women is not cultivated by drinking to excess, vomiting on city streets, or participating in public rituals of flashing to receive beads. Mardi Gras may have come unmoored from its Christian roots, from its focus on the conversion leading up to Ash Wednesday. Without its Christian foundation, Mardi Gras becomes a massive party in which the interruption of festivity on Ash Wednesday is nothing more than a blip on the radar. Every culture—both within and outside of the Church—needs to be regularly examined for this kind of sinfulness. Refusal to ask questions about what we have created, the culture that we have fostered in our parish, city, or nation, is to fall into the trap of idolatry. We adore ourselves, rather than God.

12. Culture and religion need each other.

Without a religious foundation, culture becomes a celebration of what we have created. There is no interruption by God, a source of transcendent wisdom that keeps us from closing in upon ourselves. A Mardi Gras without Ash Wednesday, Lent, and the glorious celebration of the Resurrection of Christ becomes just another party among other parties. Without the prophetic interruption of the God who created human beings for unity, members of a culture become closed off from communion with one another.

* Having read through this section on culture, list five to ten features of the culture of your parish.
* Imagine that someone outside your parish community showed up to Mass. How do you think that person would describe the culture of your parish? Would that description be different than the features you listed above?

WHAT MAKES A EUCHARISTIC CULTURE?

These twelve dimensions of culture are the building blocks for understanding what I mean by a Eucharistic culture. But there remains work to do in adapting Fr. Gallagher's description of culture to the self-giving love of Jesus Christ bestowed in the Eucharistic liturgy, what I will call a Eucharistic culture. Pope

Benedict XVI wrote a document that can help us in this adaptation. *Sacramentum Caritatis (The Sacrament of Charity)* is the apostolic exhortation written after the 2005 synod (or gathering of bishops) on the Eucharist. The document has a structure that contemplates the Eucharist as a mystery to be believed, celebrated, and lived. By *mystery*, the document means something that cannot be reduced exclusively to human reason. There are many facets to the Eucharist, and each of these facets must be contemplated if we are to understand as best as we can the love of Christ made present in the sacrifice of the Mass.

Further, Benedict's exhortation is proposing a Eucharistic culture for the renewal of the Church. Remember that Fr. Gallagher described a culture as consisting of meanings or beliefs, values, and customs or practices. The Eucharist proposes to the Church the ultimate meaning of life, which is celebrated, remembered, and made present in the Mass through Jesus Christ, and then calls us to adopt a common form of life that is thoroughly Eucharistic. Benedict XVI states this quite clearly in the opening paragraphs of *Sacramentum Caritatis (The Sacrament of Charity)*:

> In the sacrament of the Eucharist, Jesus shows us in particular the *truth about the love* that is the very essence of God. It is this evangelical truth that challenges each of us and our whole being. For this reason, the Church, which finds in the Eucharist the very center of her life, is constantly concerned to proclaim to all . . . that God is love. Precisely because Christ has become for us the food of truth,

the Church turns to every man and woman, inviting
them freely to accept God's gift.[4]

When we say that the Mass is the source and summit of Christian
life, this is what we mean. It is not that the Mass is the only thing
that is important for evangelization. Rather, the Church means
that the self-giving love of Jesus Christ given in the Mass to all
men and women is the very reason that the Church exists.

God is love. We seek to invite every person into that communion of love given by Christ Jesus. We strive to become this
love of Christ, received in the Eucharist, for the sanctification
of our neighborhoods, cities, states, our nation, and the whole
world. We long for affiliation with the Church, not because high
numbers make us look good. We long for affiliation of all men
and women with the Church because through the Church the
love of God is given for the life of the world. The Mass, therefore,
must become integral to the culture of the parish. Everything
that we believe, every practice that we perform, every norm gov-
erning our common life should be infused with the wisdom of
the Eucharistic mystery of love. When the parish does this, all
through the gift of the Holy Spirit that infuses our common life,
we have a Eucharistic culture.

For the sake of simplicity, I seek to contract Fr. Gallagher's
twelve dimensions of culture to four theses that we will then
explore more deeply in dialogue with *Sacramentum Caritatis (The
Sacrament of Charity)*. In later chapters of the book, the theses will
receive more careful attention so that the parish may enter a process of discernment relative to cultivating a Eucharistic culture.

THE FOUR THESES ABOUT EUCHARISTIC CULTURE

1. A Eucharistic culture is a human creation, which is nonetheless entirely dependent on the self-giving love of Christ in the Eucharistic mystery.

It may seem heretical initially to say that a Eucharistic culture is a human creation. After all, the Eucharistic liturgy is not defined exclusively by human activity. Rather, the Mass is that rite which remembers and makes present the love of Christ that has transformed every crack and crevice of the cosmos. As we read in *Sacramentum Caritatis (The Sacrament of Charity)*:

> In instituting the sacrament of the Eucharist, Jesus anticipates and makes present the sacrifice of the Cross and the victory of the resurrection. At the same time, he reveals that he himself is the *true* sacrificial lamb. . . . By placing his gift in this context, Jesus shows the salvific meaning of his death and resurrection, a mystery which renews history and the whole cosmos. The institution of the Eucharist demonstrates how Jesus' death, for all its violence and absurdity, became in him a supreme act of love and mankind's definitive deliverance from evil.[5]

The Mass is about what Christ has accomplished through his Death, Resurrection, and Ascension into heaven. Christ died for the salvation of the world. Death is the great problem that no human being can solve. Only God can transform the meaninglessness of death through an act of love that forever changes what it means to be human. Because Jesus Christ is the God-man, resurrected from the dead, death has no more power to slay. Love alone, the divine love revealed on the Cross, is the exclusive source of credibility.

At Mass, it is this entire Paschal Mystery—Christ's Life, Death, Resurrection, and Ascension—that is remembered and celebrated. The Church comes forth from this Eucharistic mystery—the self-giving love of Christ that gathers all men and women into this common act of worship. Despite how commonly we might hear it, liturgy is not the work of the people. It is the work of God upon the people, bringing us into a communion of love that we ourselves could never create. Liturgy is gift.

And yet, the human being is not left out of this transformation. Human beings have a role to play because the gift that Jesus gives in his very presence in the Blessed Sacrament is meant to be received by mere mortals. The gift of Christ upon the altar woos us to offer that same gift of love in return. After all, it is bread and wine—symbols of creation—that are transformed into Christ's Body and Blood. Benedict XVI notes that this transformation is a process, and we have a role to play in it. We give ourselves in return to the God who gave himself in total love. And the very shape of history, of time and space, is changed because of Jesus's love that is still offered on every altar throughout the world. Everything that is human must become divine.

> "The Eucharist draws us into Jesus' act of self-oblation. More than just statically receiving the incarnate

> Logos, we enter into the very dynamic of his self-giving." Jesus "draws us into himself." The substantial conversion of bread and wine into his body and blood introduces within creation the principle of a radical change, a sort of "nuclear fission" . . . which penetrates to the heart of all being, a change meant to set off a process that transforms reality, a process leading ultimately to the transfiguration of the entire world, to the point where God will be all in all (cf. 1 Cor 15:28).[6]

Perhaps, therefore, it is not so heretical to say that the Eucharistic culture of a parish is a human creation. It is a human creation infused with the gift of divine love, ordered toward Christ himself. It is not a personal, individual, or collective project of human beings apart from God. Rather, it is what Eastern Catholics call *synergy*: our will and God's will working together through the gift of the Spirit.

But we should remember that just because the culture of a parish is a human creation, it may not always be Eucharistic. Just because we run festivals, have a robust stewardship program, have read the latest in books on pastoral strategy, and engage in perpetual Eucharistic Adoration, does not mean that we possess a Eucharistic culture. The heart of a Eucharistic culture—even one created by a parish—is reverence. Reverence means placing the love of Christ at the center of everything we do. This reverence is learned first and foremost in the Mass, as we will see in the next chapter.

And that means cultivating a Eucharistic culture begins with the conversion of the parish toward making Christ's sacrifice of love central to our identity. We must ask hard questions about the implicit culture of our parish, such as the following:

- Do the festivals we celebrate point toward Christ, or are they simply a way of escaping the workaday world?
- Do people feel welcome in our parish, or are they greeted as if they are obstacles to our private Eucharistic encounter that we hope to enjoy all by ourselves?
- Do we talk more about ecclesiastical politics in our parish than about the love of Christ made present in the Eucharistic mystery?
- Are our Masses reverent occasions of encounter with Christ, or are they focused more on showing how remarkable we are as a community of faith?
- Is the Mass in our parish infected by the liturgy wars operative in the Church today?

These are hard questions, but this kind of collective examination of conscience is the beginning of conversion.

2. A Eucharistic culture is also a worldview, one that shapes how we approach all of reality.

Pope Benedict XVI notes that this is the real meaning of active participation in the Mass. Active participation does not just mean that we do lots of stuff during the Mass—singing our hearts out, volunteering to be lectors and ushers. It means that the Eucharist shapes our view of the world. As Benedict XVI writes, "The active participation called for by the [Second Vatican] Council must be understood in more substantial terms, on the basis of a greater awareness of the mystery being celebrated and its relationship to daily life."[7]

A culture of active participation will not be passed on all by itself during this time of cultural change—as we learned from Fr. Gallagher. We cannot presume that Catholics will just be Catholic, will participate actively in the life of the Church, because they go to Mass every Sunday (or more likely, as disaffiliation increases, once per month). It will require instead an explicit formation, an approach to catechesis that is integrally Eucharistic.

Here, we have a lot to learn. Catechesis in so many of our parishes is simply too thin to support this Eucharistic culture. Eucharistic catechesis often is reduced to explaining the doctrines of real presence and transubstantiation. This explication of these doctrines is part of what we must do, but it is not everything. The current *Directory for Catechesis* notes that there are five tasks to catechesis:

- passing on knowledge of the faith,
- initiating men and women to celebrate the mystery of Christ in the liturgy,
- attuning the heart of every Catholic to imitate Christ in every dimension of life,
- educating the believer for a life of prayer, and
- fostering a spirituality of communion in the parish community.[8]

A parish that has a Eucharistic culture would commit itself to fostering devotion to the Blessed Sacrament and to the Eucharistic way of life through each of these tasks. First, the Eucharistic mystery must be unfolded through scripture and doctrine alike, proposing to men and women (especially adults) the gift of love made available on the altar. Second, we need to infuse in men and women Eucharistic dispositions for worship, a spirit of reverence, thanksgiving, praise, and lamentation that enables the whole parish to participate more deeply in the Eucharistic sacrifice of the Mass. Third, we must recognize the ways that the moral life is in fact a Eucharistic mystery first and foremost, a response of love by men and women to the gift that we have first received upon the altar. Fourth, we must see prayer as an extension of Eucharistic gratitude, with our whole memory, understanding, and desire participating in the mystery of life through every moment of every day. Fifth, we need to nurture our love for Christian community, recognizing that this love is itself Eucharistic in shape. We love our neighbor, our fellow parishioner, because Christ has called us together to become a living mystery of divine love in the world.

Eucharistic catechesis makes explicit the worldview, as well as all the practices and traditions, which a Eucharistic culture requires. It cultivates this worldview in the context of accompanying men and women throughout their lives to take up a Eucharistic posture toward the world. It is gradual and slow, not the kind of catechesis accomplished over the course of six weeks or during childhood. Only through this slow Eucharistic catechesis,[9] building up a culture over time, can we foster the kind of active participation in the Mass that leads to the transformation of the cosmos into a space of love. A consequence of this slow process is that Eucharistic catechesis in the parish must be ordered not only toward helping children receive their First Communion but toward guiding the Eucharistic vocation of every adult to consecrate the world to Jesus Christ.

3. A Eucharistic culture is interested in every dimension of what it means to be human.

Remember that Fr. Gallagher noted that culture was about practice and meaning alike. A culture is lived through the most mundane human activities, which come to take up new meaning through initiation into that culture. When Benedict XVI speaks about the Eucharist as a mystery to be lived, this is what he means. He writes:

> Christianity's new worship includes and transfigures every aspect of life. . . . Christians, in all their actions, are called to offer true worship to God. Here the intrinsically eucharistic nature of Christian life begins to take shape. The Eucharist, since it embraces the concrete, everyday existence of the believer, makes possible, day by day, the progressive transfiguration of all those called by grace to reflect the image of the Son of God (cf. Rom 8:29ff.). There is nothing authentically human—our thoughts and affections, our words and deeds—that does not find in the sacrament of the Eucharist the form it needs to be lived to the full. Here we can see the full human

import of the radical newness brought by Christ in
the Eucharist: the worship of God in our lives cannot
be relegated to something private and individual, but
tends by its nature to permeate every aspect of our
existence. Worship pleasing to God thus becomes
a new way of living our whole life, each particular
moment of which is lifted up, since it is lived as part
of the relationship with Christ and as an offering to
God. The glory of God is the living man (cf. 1 Cor
10:31). And the life of man is the vision of God.[10]

Reading this rather long passage should function something like
a medicine for our parishes. The Eucharist is not a private activity
of a citizen, who in his or her spare time comes to Mass. To par-
take of Christ's Body and Blood is to pledge oneself to become
what is received—a sacrifice of self-giving love for the life of the
world. This "becoming" does not mean that we are to escape the
world, to develop a pleasant sectarian community of believers
apart from the hoi polloi. Catholicism is not an escape from the
human condition but instead a transfiguration. As a Catholic my
glory is to gaze in wonder upon God and, through this gaze, to
become more human. Fully human. What God created me to
be—a Eucharistic creature.

Everything that is human is to be taken up in the Eucharist,
transformed in love. A Eucharistic culture is marked by those
who see their work as part of their Eucharistic vocation. It is
made present in Eucharistic devotions that extend outside the
walls of the parish to the world. It is manifest in the homes of the

baptized—single people and families alike—who are devoted to the Eucharistic mystery of love in the context of daily life.

A parish with a Eucharistic culture intentionally cultivates a Eucharistic humanism. We invite men and women to let their imaginations be transformed, to see how their day-to-day lives are echoes of the Eucharistic mystery. Eucharistic coherency, in this instance, is not reserved exclusively for politicians. Every individual Catholic and every parish is to become Eucharistically coherent. Who we are, what we do, finds its source in the Blessed Sacrament.

4. Eucharistic culture pertains not only to persons in the parish but to the neighborhood, the city, and the nation.

As Benedict XVI writes in *Sacramentum Caritatis (The Sacrament of Charity)*, "Worship pleasing to God can never be a purely private matter, without consequences for our relationship with others: it demands a public witness to our faith."[11] The love of God that we receive in the Blessed Sacrament should lead us to love our neighbor. A Eucharistic culture is marked by a spirit of solidarity, of communion with one's neighbor. But solidarity is not a vague sense of "I feel you, bro!" Solidarity is the cultivated practice of letting the concerns of my neighbor, their joys and suffering, become part of my own.

For this reason, there are always public consequences to the celebration of a Eucharistic culture. Parishes must recognize this. Upholding the dignity of each person is not an optional dimension of Catholic life, the sort of thing we do if we are interested in such things. If there is racism in our neighborhoods, if pregnant women do not receive sufficient support, and if there is massive ecological damage to the city, then the neighborhood itself needs to be part of Eucharistic revival. The parish is not, after all, a building. It is a geographic boundary in which every human being in that parish should know their Eucharistic dignity. In this way, the Eucharist is always a political sacrament, not in a partisan sense, but in a healthy, united one. The Eucharist should contribute to the flourishing of the whole *polis* or city.

These last two dimensions of the Eucharistic culture of a parish point toward the ultimate reason to cultivate this kind of culture in a parish. The goal is the renewal of all cultures, to create spaces of sacrificial love in the world. Members of Catholic parishes are not only consumers of the Eucharist, enjoying private spiritual experiences. We are creators of culture, abiding within communities, who are called to foster a world that is increasingly Eucharistic.

- Look back at the list you made on page 14 of the various features that define the culture of your parish.
- Do you see the four aspects of a Eucharistic culture in your parish? Are there areas where your parish requires a conversion to foster a new culture?

CONCLUSION

In this chapter, I have outlined four facets of Eucharistic culture in dialogue with Pope Benedict XVI's *Sacramentum Caritatis (The Sacrament of Charity)*. But articulating this culture is only the first part of beginning a process of discernment. Carefully attending to these four dimensions of Eucharistic culture, while inviting parishes to undertake a process of Eucharistic discernment, is the purpose of this book. The remaining chapters will say a bit more about each facet of this culture, suggesting ways for parishes to undertake a process of self-examination in order to foster this Eucharistic culture in the parish.

2.

A CULTURE OF EUCHARISTIC REVERENCE

It may seem counterintuitive to say that a Eucharistic culture—one that cultivates the unity of the Church and the *polis* or city—should begin with reverence. After all, the word *reverence* is often employed in the context of the half-century liturgy wars that so often dominate Church life.

I certainly understand this fear. Since 2010, I have served as the academic director of the Notre Dame Center for Liturgy. In this role, I have seen the fallout from liturgy wars in parishes and dioceses throughout the United States and beyond. At national gatherings, I have heard prominent liturgical leaders mock young traditional seminarians who are rigid and supposedly care only about the wearing of cassocks and the celebration of the Latin Mass. The revival of practices such as Eucharistic Adoration and Benediction of the Blessed Sacrament is viewed suspiciously by many professional liturgists who see these practices as returning to preconciliar devotional life. On the other hand, I frequently receive emails from self-identified traditionalists who tell me that it is the Novus Ordo (that is, the reformed Mass of the Second Vatican Council) that is the source of every ecclesial and social decline. The *irreverence* of the "New Mass" and all those liberal liturgists are the problem.

But let us take a step back from the liturgical conflicts since Vatican II and attend to the meaning of reverence. In Latin, the word *reverence* can be translated as either *religio* or *veneratio*. The word *religion* does not simply mean a coherent system of beliefs but means a posture of awe or wonder before God. The religious act commences with reverent, awe-filled worship of God. God is at the center of what we do, not us.

In Catholicism, reverence recognizes that what we do in the liturgical act is real. In contrast to the religion of the aesthete—someone who simply enjoys the experience of worship because it is beautiful—reverence is about the deadly serious business of salvation. It is the very real worship of God that makes possible the sanctification of men and women. Yes, such worship often is both enjoyable and lovely. But it is also serious because the salvation of men and women is at stake.

The Roman Catholic theologian Fr. Romano Guardini discusses the beauty and yet deadly seriousness of liturgical reverence in his *The Spirit of the Liturgy*. He writes:

> The Church has not built up the *Opus Dei* for the pleasure of forming beautiful symbols, choice language, and graceful, stately gestures, but she has done it—in so far as it is not completely devoted to the worship of God—for the sake of our desperate spiritual need. It is to give expression to the events of the

Christian's inner life: the assimilation, through the Holy Ghost, of the life of the creature to the life of God in Christ; the actual and genuine rebirth of the creature into a new existence; the development and nourishment of its life, its stretching forth from God in the Blessed Sacrament and the means of grace, towards God in prayer and sacrifice; and all this in the continued mystic renewal of Christ's life in the course of the ecclesiastical year. The fulfillment of all these processes by the set forms of language, gestures, and instruments, their revelation, teaching, accomplishment and acceptance by the faithful, together constitute the liturgy. We see, then, that it is primarily concerned with reality, with the approach of a real creature to a real God, and with the profoundly real and serious matter of redemption.[1]

Liturgy is not playacting or developing a disinterested delight in the symbols of Catholic culture. When women and men approach the liturgy, our lives are being transformed. We are learning to live a new life in Christ. Nothing that we have can be understood or lived apart from Jesus.

Recognizing the "realness" of worship as an encounter with the triune God is reverence. Reverence means that everything we do in the act of worship points toward the reality of God and not our own ideas about self-improvement. In this sense, there are all sorts of ways that a parish's celebration of the Eucharist might be irreverent. A parish that celebrates the reformed liturgy of the Second Vatican Council might be irreverent. The parish could include a presider who yells the various prayers as if he is reading a phone book in the middle of Times Square. A cantor could shower all attention upon himself or herself—"Look at me; I just sang 'O Holy Night.'" A parish's architecture might look more like a shopping mall than the place where the serious business of salvation unfolds.

But even a supposedly "reverent" liturgy can become irreverent. I have attended liturgies celebrated according to the 1962 *Missal* (what before Pope Francis's recent *motu proprio* was called the "Extraordinary Form" or colloquially the "Latin Mass"). As the ministers processed from the sanctuary, everyone pulled out their smartphones to take a picture of the procession. In this moment, the act of worship became about the gathered community's rejoicing in the Instagram-worthiness of a Solemn Pontifical Mass rather than their gratitude for the Eucharistic Lord.

A Eucharistic culture in a parish must be marked by a reverence that places God at the center of the act of worship. In a Eucharistic parish, during Mass, we are offering our lives as a return sacrifice of love to the triune God who created, redeems, and gathers all men and women into a communion of love that surpasses all understanding.

This approach to reverence means that enculturation of various traditions is a possibility. During my graduate-school days in Boston, our weekly liturgy at Boston College sometimes included processions drawn from the Zaire Rite. The Zaire Rite is an adaptation of the Roman Rite of the Mass, approved in 1988, for celebration. At our Wednesday Mass, an African Catholic would process in with the Book of the Gospels, enthroning it in the context of a dance that drew our attention to the beauty of the book. Now this dance was not like what we might find at a local club or even a ballet hall. The body was used to draw attention to the presence of our Lord Jesus Christ, who speaks in the Gospel. The dance was an act of reverence because the embodied practice was focused on God rather than on us or the dancer.

The Roman Rite of the Mass allows for such diversity. Hymns may be sung instead of the chants given in the *Roman Missal.* These hymns will likely reflect the cultural identities of the worshipping communities. The architecture of the building may take on different forms depending on location. A parish church in San Antonio may be inspired by the missions, for example, while the Basilica at the University of Notre Dame is built using bricks from the lakes on campus. The language of the rites may be different, allowing for celebration in Vietnamese, Spanish, English, Polish, and many other languages.

But there is a danger with such enculturation when the focus becomes us rather than God. Authentic enculturation always depends on reverence, a sense that we are encountering a real God who wants to change our lives in a genuine way in the Eucharistic liturgy. The liturgy cannot be changed because we want to be creative. The rites of the Church are the source of our common Eucharistic culture. The language of the Eucharistic Prayers ought to form all Catholics in thinking about the Eucharist as a sacrifice of love that brings men and women into the Communion of Saints through the real presence of Jesus Christ dwelling among us. Reverence means we give ourselves over to the language of the rites, being shaped by the common culture of the whole Church rather than the private ideologies of the priest or local parish.

But how do we know if we celebrate the liturgy in an enculturated albeit reverent way within our parishes? Parishes possess a
Eucharistic culture of reverence when we counteract banality by

- remembering why we are gathering in the first place,
- praying rather than reading or saying parts of the Mass,
- leaving room for contemplation and silence during the
  Eucharistic liturgy,
- understanding how the body matters in worship, and
- allowing Eucharistic devotion to permeate parish life.

After you read more about each of these five dimensions of
enculturated Eucharistic reverence through what follows in this
chapter, you will be ready to download from the McGrath Institute's website resources to help you assess the reverence of your
parish liturgies—preferably within the context of a Eucharistic
retreat.

LITURGICAL BANALITY AND
THE KERYGMA

The Mass cannot be celebrated in a banal way if it is to be reverent. *Banality* is a word that means something is unoriginal or
exceedingly commonplace. The truly banal is boring, not worth
giving our attention to in the first place. A banal speech, for
example, might be one full of clichés. It says something to us
that we already know in a way that does not attract our attention.
Coaches in press conferences often speak in banalities. "The better

team won." "I'm just so impressed with our guys' performance." "This is going to be a tough one."

People find the Mass boring when it is celebrated in a banal way, as if what we are doing is entirely unoriginal or unremarkable. In the Eucharistic liturgy, we are encountering the total self-giving love of the Word-made-flesh. God dwells among us in the scriptures, in the assembly, and most especially in the Eucharistic presence of our Lord. A banal liturgy yawns about this fact, not quite recognizing the significance of what is happening in the liturgy.

Liturgical banality must be healed through a remembering of what we are doing in the liturgy. Pope Francis has often spoken about a return to the first proclamation or the *kerygma* (a Greek word meaning "proclamation") as essential to the task of evangelization. In *Evangelii Gaudium (The Joy of the Gospel)*, he writes:

> On the lips of the catechist the first proclamation must ring out over and over: "Jesus Christ loves you; he gave his life to save you; and now he is living at your side every day to enlighten, strengthen and free you." This first proclamation is called "first" not because it exists at the beginning and can then be forgotten or replaced by other more important things. It is first in a qualitative sense because it is the principal proclamation, the one which we must hear again and again in different ways.[2]

Notice what the Holy Father is saying: the first proclamation is everything for the Catholic. It is the fact that Jesus Christ is the Son of the Father, who gave himself over for the life of the world.

Here and now, Jesus Christ as the resurrected Lord is present to me. No matter what I am going through, Jesus is there to accompany me. This is the source of a Christian's joy: my life has meaning because of Jesus.

Liturgical banality is a forgetfulness that what we celebrate at Mass is the presence of Jesus Christ to us here and now. Through the Mass, we encounter the Life, Death, Resurrection, and Ascension of Jesus in this time and space. We are not just reading a script. We are not fulfilling an obligation for Sunday Mass as clergy or the lay faithful. The Lord of history is coming to dwell among us in our communion with one another as members of the Church, healing our wounds and bringing us into a deeper relationship with the Father through the power of the Holy Spirit.

Liturgies become banal when we forget what God is doing for us in the act of worship, when we forget the story that matters. Jesus Christ has died, risen, ascended, and now seeks to draw us to the right hand of the Father. Every word and gesture of the Mass is intended to bring us into deeper union with Jesus Christ, who has come to save me, to save you, to save us.

For this reason, avoiding liturgical banality begins with reencountering the kerygma. Is my parish sufficiently aware (or desirous) of an encounter with Jesus Christ? If the parish is not, no mission statement or pastoral consultants will be of assistance. We must get serious about what is at stake, the salvation of men and women, through bending the knee before our Eucharistic Lord.

This requires a conversion of the Church. The Church is not a bureaucratic entity or a democratic society of people who just happen to believe in the same thing. We are those convoked by a story of a love beyond all telling, a community of memory that presents to the world the love of God made flesh in Jesus Christ.

Practically, the conversion toward the kerygma in the parish can start by simply reflecting on the name of your church. Parish names mean something. Julianne Stanz, who works in the Diocese of Green Bay, has told me that she often wonders why parishes do not attend more to their parish patron before working to compose a new mission statement. The parish patron of a Church is a prophetic reminder to the parish that our story is connected to the larger story of divine love revealed in Jesus Christ. We are communities grounded in the proclamation of Jesus Christ. We cannot forget this.

PRAYING, NOT TALKING

There are lots of ways to communicate the importance of our relationship with Jesus Christ, to show everyone who walks through our parish doors that Jesus is the reason for our gathering. Praying instead of speaking the words of the liturgy is one such way.

We all know the difference between a priest who prays the Eucharistic Prayer and one who reads the text as if he is an announcer at a baseball game. The former is speaking to the Father through the Son by means of the Holy Spirit rather than reading to the gathered assembly. He has contemplated the prayers before he begins Mass instead of opening the book minutes before the liturgy starts. He has spent time before Mass not simply running about but preparing to celebrate the Mass, silencing his inner thoughts so that he can offer this prayer for the gathered assembly.

The reformed liturgy of the Second Vatican Council, because it made so many prayers public, required more of the priest than ever before. The *Roman Missal*—the official prayer book of the Church—knows how difficult it is for the priest to pray this text. Therefore, the *Missal* encourages the priest to chant the prayers of the Mass. By chanting the Eucharistic Prayer, the priest must slow down, attending to each of the words in the text. The link between singing and speech in chant is important to many religious traditions and not just Catholicism. Chanting is an elevated form of speech, drawing our attention to what we are saying to God.

Another way in which the priest prays rather than speaks texts is through attending to his bodily posture in prayer. Some priests have developed bad habits in presiding. They fiddle their hands when they are sitting. They constantly shift feet, rock, or sway, never staying still. They keep looking down at their watch during Mass or joke with the altar servers rather than pay attention to the Gospel. These gestures, often unintentional, rip us away from prayer, banalizing the liturgy for the baptized faithful and the ordained priest alike. None of this means that the priest should be stuffy or joyless. But at the same time, he is offering the sacrifice of the Mass, not attending a baseball game with a bunch of his friends.

Here, something must be said about the direction the priest faces during the Eucharistic Prayer. Over the last fifteen years, this has become a controversy. For much of the Church's history, the priest has prayed the Eucharistic Prayer toward the liturgical east.[3] This posture, called *ad orientem* or "toward the east," can still be seen in Eastern Catholic churches. The eastern direction of this prayer is important. Catholics throughout time have understood the east as the direction in which Christ would return. Turning toward the liturgical east (even if it's the western part of a Church) directs our attention toward the advent of Jesus Christ.

Many times, this posture is interpreted incorrectly as the priest turning his back on the people. Especially after the reforms of Vatican II—where the Eucharistic Prayer is prayed aloud—this is a misunderstanding. In this posture the priest and the people alike turn toward the liturgical east, addressing the Father through the Son, in the unity of the Holy Spirit. Both priest and people take up the same posture in prayer, turning to God together.

Since the Second Vatican Council, it has become normative in most parishes for the priest to pray the Eucharistic Prayer *versus populum* or "toward the people." Just like *ad orientem* prayer, there is wisdom here if the posture is understood correctly. Facing the people is not just a gesture expressing the priest's familiarity with the people. It is not a poor man's reenactment of the Last Supper. Instead, the priest and the people alike are gazing upon the altar where Jesus Christ becomes present in the Eucharistic elements. *Versus populum* worship is reminiscent of the book of Revelation in which the saints look together upon the Lamb once slain.

In the reformed rites of the Church, both postures are possible and can draw us more deeply into prayer. I have attended Masses in hotel meeting rooms, where spaces absent of all obvious sacredness were transformed the moment that Fr. Joshua

Johnson—a Catholic priest of the Diocese of Baton Rouge—turned toward the liturgical east. I have also been to Mass at my parish, St. Pius X, and seen how the eyes of Msgr. Bill Schooler and the entire assembly are directed in wonder at the Host lifted high for all to behold. The crucifix on the altar is contemplated by Msgr. Schooler throughout the Eucharistic Prayer. He does not look up every thirty seconds to look at us, as if we are awaiting his eye contact to make sure that we are recognized. We are all praying together.

Priests are not the only people who speak words during the liturgy. Lectors in parishes also are invited to pray. This may be surprising to us. The minimum requirement for being a lector in most parishes is the capacity to read a text and the accompanying *Lectionary* workbook (to make sure that we pronounce the words correctly). I have attended numerous lector trainings in parishes where nearly all emphasis is on processing with the Book of the Gospels and learning to work with the microphone at the ambo. But, like the priest, the lector is called to pray the scriptures rather than just read them. A good lector should begin preparation with savoring the Sunday *Lectionary* texts. If the lector loves the text that he is reading, the text will be proclaimed in a way that manifests this love to all who are gathered.

The same is true for extraordinary ministers of Holy Communion. This ministry cannot be reduced to standing in the proper place and developing the right technique for placing the Host in the hands of the communicant. When the extraordinary minister of Holy Communion holds up the Eucharistic Lord and proclaims, "The Body of Christ," the minister should be praying.

This is Christ's Body, the presence of Jesus Christ dwelling among us. He wants to give himself to you. He wants to give himself to me. What a wondrous mystery to behold and to delight in. If the extraordinary minister does not delight in this mystery, then the proclamation of the host as Christ's Body will come off as banal. It will just be what we say when we pass out Communion, nothing more. "Amen." Yawn.

Of course, the entire assembly is involved in praying the Mass and not just the ordained and other ministers. All the faithful need formation to pray the words of Holy Mass, to let our "Amen" ring true rather than function as pro forma speech. This comprehensive formation will be addressed in the following chapter. But if the priest and the liturgical ministers pray the Mass, the entire People of God will be more likely to delight in their parts. *Lift up your hearts. We lift them up to the Lord!*

ROOM FOR CONTEMPLATION AND SILENCE

Integral to promoting a culture of reverence is learning to be comfortable with silence. If you speak to those attracted to the pre–Vatican II Mass, they often tell you that what they love the most is the silence. They feel as if Mass is truly prayed—that is, they are given space to contemplate the wondrous mystery of divine love.

We must admit that many post-conciliar Masses are verbose. Now, there is never going to be absolute silence in a vibrant parish. Babies and kids will scream out or try to run around.

Parish announcements must be read. But none of this requires the amount of speech that we typically experience at Mass.

The priest, seeking to cultivate a culture of reverence, will need to examine the frequency of his own speaking. Yes, the reformed Mass allows for the priest to introduce the Mass of the day. But many priests speak too much during the first moments of Mass. They give an extensive history of the saint of the day, providing a mini lecture. I often hear priests start Mass by saying, "Just as we always do, let us begin in the name of the Father, the Son, and the Holy Spirit." What does this interpolation add to our prayer? Do people need to be reminded that we always begin Mass in the name of the Father, the Son, and the Holy Spirit? Have they forgotten since last week? No! This is unnecessary speech. Beginning with a brief silence would do far more for fostering a reverent liturgy than telling everyone that we have prayed this part of the Mass before.

The priest should also integrate silence into parts of the reformed Mass where silence is encouraged. Instead of rushing into the Collect or opening prayer, let there be a moment of silence after the priest says, "Let us pray." Rather than rush through the Eucharistic Prayer as if one is trying to beat a world speaking record, the priest can take his time praying. Let moments of silence come into play during the various parts of the Eucharistic Prayer, as I have often heard the liturgist Fr. Paul Turner say. Let there be silence after we have received the Body and Blood of Christ rather than more organ, piano, or guitar music. Let explanations in the liturgy be very brief, if necessary at all. Is it truly necessary to explain the procedure for coming forward to receive the Body and Blood of Christ every week?

Silence, after all, is integral to our human experience. When a friend of mine is telling me about something tragic that has happened to him or her, the reverent thing to do is to be silent with that person. When I held my son for the first time, I did not let a flood of words interrupt my gaze. It was enough to behold the mystery of new life, of this life that I would now be responsible for. Silence in these instances show us that something wonderful is happening that is worth contemplating.

Contemplation can be defined simply as beholding that which is most real. I am silent before the tragedy of my friend, because what I see is the reality of human suffering. No speech can replace that silence. It is not the time to give a speech on how to deal with suffering. The silence speaks volumes. The same is true with the birth of my son. In silence, I was able to contemplate the reality of my son as gift.

We are very uncomfortable with silence in late modern life, used to noise wherever we go. Allowing for spaces of silence at Mass will not only create more reverent liturgies. It will offer a medicine that we deeply crave—time away from the noise.

THE BODY MATTERS

One of the consequences of our obsession with words in the liturgy is that we sometimes forget that reverence is first caught rather than taught. Let me explain. Many First Communion programs try their best to teach second graders everything they need to know about the Eucharist. They need to know the scriptural foundations, the Eucharistic doctrines of the Church, and the parts of the Mass.

What we forget is that a culture of Eucharistic reverence starts with the body. My son learned that the Eucharist was integral to the life of our family and that Jesus Christ was present in the Blessed Sacrament not through instruction in a classroom. He learned it because we went to Mass. He discovered it because my wife and I taught him (and later his sister) to genuflect before the tabernacle. We taught both our kids to look at churches with wonder, delighting in the presence of the sheep painted on the walls, suggesting that we too are sheep of so gracious a shepherd who wants to guard and feed us. He learned our love of the Blessed Sacrament, the beauty of Jesus's presence, because we closed our eyes when we sang the *Sanctus* at Mass or when we received our precious Lord in Holy Communion. Reverence was caught through the body, rather than taught using more words.

Now, I'm a theologian. I spend much of my life using words to teach Christian doctrine to undergraduates at the University of Notre Dame. There is a time and space for such teaching—and as my undergraduates would tell you, I take full advantage of those moments.

But Eucharistic reverence in my life always comes back to how I use my body in worship. I caught it first. My grandmother taught me to hold my hands together when I prayed. My grandfather taught me to kneel before the Blessed Sacrament. My Mexican friends taught me to say the words of St. Thomas in the Gospel of John quietly to myself during the Eucharistic Prayer, as the Host was held up to behold: "My Lord and my God." The body matters.

This is the real reason that art, architecture, and music matter in worship. While we will look more closely at these in the next chapter, it is enough now to remind us that we need art, architecture, and music because we possess bodies. I do not worship an abstract God in the Eucharistic liturgy but Jesus Christ, who took flesh, died upon the Cross, and was raised from the dead. That's why I need a crucifix to behold at Mass. Similarly, when I go to the Basilica of Sacred Heart at Notre Dame, the stained glass windows of the saints represent for me the presence of the communion of holy ones who worship the Lamb once slain. It's a reminder for me that Mass is never just a celebration of a single parish community. During COVID-19, when I was unable to be at Mass or behold the presence of Jesus in the Blessed Sacrament, I still had the words of the *Tantum Ergo* that I had learned to sing as a young boy at my parish church in East Tennessee. Simply singing those words seemed to bring me into the presence of Jesus Christ.

Thus, attending to the art in our churches is integral to fostering an embodied reverence. Leading up to Vatican II, a fallacy developed. Namely, the simpler the church, the better. I have been in churches with too much art, lacking any unity. But at least these churches presumed that when I am worshipping God, I am going to use my body. I am going to look at statues, light candles, and enter communion with the saints. Because I have a body, I need stuff.

After the Council, what happened was an iconoclasm that got rid of stuff. Liturgical worship became more about sincerity rather than proposing a divine world mediated to us through matter. We did not need a cross to behold, stained glass windows, statues, or music to wonder at. What we needed was a heart disposed to worship. But this is a mistake. We are not monks, marinating all day in sacred scripture. The stuff of worship is what makes Catholicism so real to people.

For this reason, art, architecture, and music are privileged places for enculturated reverence. I have discovered the reality of God at Masses in Spanish, English, Polish, and French. God is not made manifest only in Gothic churches. So much of enculturation is in the presence of Marian images from Poland, Mexico, or Ireland. Murals on walls show us part of our history.

But we must simultaneously acknowledge that art, architecture, and music can also be experienced as sources of banality or what in art is often called kitsch. Art, architecture, and music is kitschy when it is formulaic, when it does exactly what you expect for it to do. We must face the fact, especially relative to music, that much of what we use at Mass is at least a bit kitschy. Many psalms and hymns sound more like ditties from a commercial than the Communion of Saints adoring the Lamb once slain. The subtle communication in this kitschy music is that what we are doing at this Mass is no more important than the music that plays in a commercial. Our bodies recognize this before our minds.

In saying this, I am not claiming that we must sing only Renaissance polyphony in Latin. Rather, we must acknowledge that the music we sing in a parish should lead us into an encounter with the reality of God, wooing us to lift up our hearts to participate in heavenly worship. William Byrd's *Ave verum corpus* is a musical piece that does this. In this classic text professing faith in the reality of Christ's Eucharistic presence on the altar, Byrd forms us in Eucharistic reverence. Before us is the true Body of Christ, born of the Virgin Mary, whose side was pierced upon the Cross and produced blood and water. As we eat and drink Christ's Body and Blood, this is the true Body that we receive. Byrd's incorporation of various chants on top of each other, his use of dynamics (soft and loud), and the way that he addresses Jesus Christ present upon the altar invite us into an embodied reverence before the Blessed Sacrament.

But we do not have to rely on Byrd alone for this reverence. I have attended Benediction of the Blessed Sacrament where we have sung the music of the band Third Day, the haunting melodies of contemporary composers, and the praise-and-worship music of the evangelical Hillsong churches. What makes such music "not kitschy" is how it speaks about God. We do not sing about ourselves. We do not reduce God to something that is immediately comprehensible. The mystery of love is encountered as we sing Third Day's "Agnus Dei / Worthy," acknowledging that God is holy, the King of Kings, and the Lord of Lords. The reality of Christ's presence in the Blessed Sacrament is made manifest when we join our voices with a contemporary setting of the classic hymn "Holy, Holy, Holy." In these acts of singing or listening to poetic compositions, it is our flesh-and-blood selves that are placed before the living presence of God. Music is where we come to see the reality of God.

A Eucharistic culture of reverence remembers, therefore, the importance of the body in worship by being critical of banality and kitsch in our art, architecture, and music. If we want to recultivate love of the Blessed Sacrament, it is here where we have the most work to do.

Eucharistic Devotion

Lastly, a culture of Eucharistic reverence in a parish will cultivate Eucharistic reverence. This reverence is best developed in our celebration of the Mass. We should pray the texts of the Mass, take up a posture of silence before the mystery of love, and regularly use our bodies in worship. But there are additional ways to renew Eucharistic devotion.

First, we should be attentive to the language that we use when speaking about the Eucharist. What we encounter at Mass is the very person of Jesus Christ made present. Through the power of the Spirit in the Eucharistic Prayer, bread and wine become Body and Blood. The term *real presence* is ultimately an acknowledgment of the personal presence of our Lord dwelling among us. We should not refer to the Blessed Sacrament as "it" or as an "object." If priests and catechists use this language, everyone else will pick it up. Many Eucharistic hymns, in fact, do use this language when referring to the Blessed Sacrament, failing to address the Host as the beloved presence of our Lord.

We should therefore speak of this presence in a way that recognizes the extraordinary gift offered to us by Jesus. We receive at Mass the bread of life, manna from heaven, and angelic food and drink. We adore our Lord at Mass, eating and drinking at the supper of the Lamb. The more that we use elevated language that is personal to refer to the Eucharist, the more that devotion will be fostered in the parish. Maybe it is time to relearn that most beautiful of profession of faith before Jesus's presence (often prayed after Communion), "O Sacrament most holy, O Sacrament divine, all praise and all thanksgiving be every moment Thine."

Fostering a culture of Eucharistic reverence includes worship of the Blessed Sacrament outside of Mass. Another misconception that developed after Vatican II was the unimportance of Eucharistic devotion in 40 Hour Adoration, Benediction of the Blessed Sacrament, Holy Hours before the Lord in the tabernacle, and processions of the Blessed Sacrament on Corpus Christi and during times of harvest. Yes, liturgical reform wanted to emphasize how important the Mass was for Catholic life. As we will see in the next chapter, we are meant to pray the liturgy. But this prayer extends outside of the Mass.

Eucharistic Adoration and Benediction of the Blessed Sacrament are not denials of the importance of the sacrifice of praise that the Church offers in the Eucharistic liturgy proper. Rather, they are extensions of gratitude, of love before the Eucharistic presence of our Lord, who does not disappear after we depart on Sunday morning from our parish church. He remains here, dwelling among us. Stopping by a parish church to sit in the presence of our Lord is an act of devotion that increases love for the Eucharist. Likewise, Benediction of the Blessed Sacrament formed the Church to acknowledge the personal presence of Jesus in the Eucharist. In the Divine Praises, we do not speak of God abstractly. We praise the holy name of Jesus, his Sacred Heart, and his precious Blood. We sing the hymns of St. Thomas Aquinas, especially the *Tantum Ergo*, before the presence of Jesus.

It is time for the Church to stop seeing a clash between Adoration of the Blessed Sacrament outside of Mass and the celebration of the Eucharistic liturgy. Both are ordered toward fostering reverent love for Jesus Christ dwelling among us. The Eucharist, of course, is meant to be received. The Blessed Sacrament is food for the journey. But the Eucharist is food for the journey because it is the presence of our Lord dwelling among us. Gazing with gratitude upon this gift only increases the desire for loving reception of our Lord. We are meant to taste and to see the goodness of the Lord (see Psalm 34:9).

CONCLUSION

Eucharistic reverence is not a rehashing of the liturgy wars that have embroiled US Catholicism over the last fifty years. It is not a return to Latin (nor, for that matter, is it a denial of Latin's importance). Rather, liturgical reverence is about celebrating the liturgy in a way that is joyfully serious. The five aspects of reverence just explored correspond in the accompanying online resources with an invitation for a parish to undertake a process of self-examination. Do we celebrate the Eucharist reverently as a Church of many cultures?

For in Eucharistic worship, we receive the Body and Blood of Jesus Christ as we offer the sacrifice of praise that brings the Church into existence. That's right. The Church is not a bureaucracy but consists of men and women called to communion with the Lord and one another. Eucharistic formation of the faithful should be dedicated to fostering an active participation in the Mass in this deep sense. It is this integral Eucharistic formation that is the topic of the next chapter.

- What are your first reactions to these five dimensions of an enculturated reverence at Mass? Would you say, upon first reaction, that your parish celebrates the liturgy in an enculturated reverent manner?
- Download the suggested retreat and day of discernment on the Notre Dame Center for Liturgy's website on enculturated reverence. Send any questions or thoughts that you have about running this retreat to ndcl@nd.edu.

3.

A CULTURE OF INTEGRAL EUCHARISTIC FORMATION

Eucharistic catechesis in the Roman Catholic Church is lacking. This is not because sacramental formation for First Communion is poor. In fact, sacramental preparation is often the best catechesis that a child will receive. My son's reception of the Blessed Sacrament was marked by retreats, the reading of scripture, and a contemplation of the various parts of the liturgy. His formation was an invitation for me to return to deeper Eucharistic faith.[1]

Eucharistic catechesis is lacking because it is not meant exclusively for second graders receiving their First Holy Communion. Eucharistic catechesis is a lifelong project in which we learn to participate actively in the Mass, including receiving our Lord Jesus Christ in the Blessed Sacrament. This kind of Eucharistic catechesis must be integral. *Integral* means that which is complete, essential, and fundamental. An integral Eucharistic catechesis presumes that we are fostering mature disciples in the parish who live out their Eucharistic identity as baptized priests, prophets, and royal figures meant to consecrate the world to Jesus Christ. A disintegrated Eucharistic formation will attend only to child and not to the maturation of adults in their Eucharistic faith.

The problem with Eucharistic catechesis is really a dilemma with catechesis in general. Namely, we think about catechesis exclusively as explaining or presenting various doctrines for the assent primarily of a young person. The verb *catechize* is regularly used in this manner. If people are not coming to Mass, then we must *catechize* the youth to fix that problem. In the meantime, our parishes remain bereft of the kind of adult faith formation necessary for cultivating a Eucharistic people.

This typical approach to catechesis is too thin, as the 2020 *Directory for Catechesis* reminds us:

> At the center of every process of catechesis is the living encounter with Christ. "Accordingly, the definitive aim of catechesis is to put people not only in touch but in communion, in intimacy with Jesus Christ: only he can lead us to the love of the Father in the Spirit and make us share in the life of the Holy Trinity." Communion with Christ is the center of the Christian life, and as a result the center of catechetical action. Catechesis is oriented toward forming persons who get to know Jesus Christ and his Gospel of liberating salvation even better; who live a profound encounter with him and who choose his own way of life and his very sentiments (cf. Phil 2:5), striving to realize, in the historical situation in which they live, the mission of Christ, which is the proclamation of the kingdom of God.[2]

Notice how comprehensive catechesis is supposed to be. We seek to invite men and women into a relationship with Jesus Christ, which is salvific. They reflect on the meaning of their lives as an encounter with Jesus, choosing to follow him more closely every day. Through discipleship, those who receive catechesis over the course of their lifetimes gradually extend the reign of God to every crack and crevice of the cosmos.

The almost exclusive focus on childhood Eucharistic catechesis causes us to forget how comprehensive Eucharistic formation should be. We are called to bestow the best catechesis for adults and not just for children. A Eucharistic culture will form mature men and women in full, conscious, and active participation in the Eucharistic life of the Church. Only then will parishes possess an integral Eucharistic formation for the sake of renewing the world in Jesus Christ.

• Before continuing, think about adult catechesis at your parish. What kind of formation takes place? Would you describe this formation as integral? Why or why not?

CATECHESIS, ADULTHOOD, AND ACTIVE PARTICIPATION

The claim that catechesis is needed for adults goes against so many of our assumptions about religious education. Except for the initiation of adults during Easter, we presume that most parish catechesis is ordered toward children. This catechesis is meant to pass on the rudiments of faith to the future generation, culminating in the reception of the Sacrament of Confirmation. After that, there will be occasional, albeit irregular, moments of catechesis for other sacraments.

Now, don't mistake me. The catechesis of children is important for the Church. We must invite children—especially those receiving their First Communion—to understand the gift they are receiving. Approaches such as Catechesis of the Good Shepherd have shown us that young children are capable of mature insights about God, if they are taught in a way that is appropriate for the young child, while still grounded in scripture and liturgy alike.[3]

Further, experience testifies to the importance of a childhood encounter with the Eucharist for later adult faith. My love of the Blessed Sacrament began when my grandmother and grandfather began to take me to the 7:00 a.m. Mass at St. David's Parish in south Florida. I will always remember standing outside St. David's before my First Communion, bedecked in a white suit in the hot Florida sun. This day is as vivid to me as my wedding day.

With these caveats, readers should know that scholars of catechesis have rediscovered the importance of adulthood in religious formation over the last twenty-five years.[4] Such importance is underlined by the documents of the Church. The paradigm of all catechesis is not children gathered in a classroom. Instead, it is the adult catechumenate where men and women are initiated into the fullness of Christian life through instruction, periods of discernment, retreats, common prayer, and the liturgical life of the Church.

What does the Church say about adult catechesis? And why is it so important? The 2020 *Directory for Catechesis* states:

> Catechesis with adults is therefore configured as a personal and community learning process, aimed at the acquisition of a mentality of faith. . . . Its main objective is therefore the formation and maturation of life in the Spirit, according to the principles of gradualness and progressiveness, so that the Gospel message may be received in its transformative dynamism and thus become capable of making its mark on personal and social life. In the final analysis, catechesis with adults reaches it goal when it makes the adults themselves capable of taking their own experience of faith in hand and desirous of continuing to journey onward and to grow.[5]

Adult catechesis is important because most of our lives are lived in this stage of adulthood. We are initiated into Catholic faith, but that is not the end. Our vocation as baptized sons and daughters of Jesus is to consecrate every dimension of life. In our work, our friendships, our marriages, and our jobs, we are called to be missionary disciples who love unto the end. This is not easy, and we cannot do it all by ourselves.

Being an adult is hard. My undergraduates know this, and therefore they often refer to paying bills and making large commitments as "adulting." In the United States, people "become" adults today often in their mid-to-late twenties. We then have careers, families, and big decisions to make. As Catholics, we are meant to make all these decisions as baptized sons and daughters.

Will I take another job? How will I raise my kids? Where should they go to school? How do I find meaning in my life, even in those mundane of moments? Adult questions that require an adult catechesis, one that requires increasing union with Jesus.

Adulthood, in this way, is really defined by a *complete* participation in the mission of Christ. In the first chapter of this book, I spoke about Pope Benedict XVI's understanding of active participation. If you remember, Pope Benedict considers active participation to be a deeper participation in the mystery of Jesus Christ through the celebration of the Mass. *Actuosa participatio* (actual participation) is ordered toward attuning the body, the mind, and the heart in the act of worship. What we do with our body, we contemplate in our mind, and we love in our heart.

This approach to active participation is hard for many contemporary Westerners. Fr. Romano Guardini—whom we encountered in the last chapter—raised this concern in 1964 to the German bishops. He wrote to the bishops, who were immersed in questions linked to liturgical renewal raised by Vatican II:

> The question is whether the wonderful opportunities now open to the liturgy will achieve their full realization: whether we shall be satisfied with just removing anomalies, taking new situations into account, giving better instruction on the meaning of ceremonies and liturgical vessels or whether we shall relearn a forgotten way of doing things and recapture lost attitudes.[6]

Here, Guardini is saying that liturgical renewal is not only about understanding what happens in the Mass. It is about learning a new way of being human through liturgical celebration. Romano Guardini asks whether we can take up a posture of adoration, of loving contemplation, of joyful celebration and union with Christ, in every dimension of our lives. Simply put, he is calling us toward an adult participation in the Eucharistic life.

A Eucharistic catechesis in the Church will focus on cultivating active participation—in this integral sense—within the People of God. As the *Directory for Catechesis* highlights, the Church cultivates an active participation in the mystery of Christ in five ways: (1) teaching knowledge of faith, (2) educating into liturgical dispositions, (3) forming one for life in Christ, (4) initiating the Catholic into the art of prayer, and (5) fostering community life.

1. Integral Eucharistic catechesis will teach knowledge of the Eucharistic dimensions of Catholic faith.

The Eucharistic mystery in Catholicism is everywhere in sacred scripture and sacred Tradition. Active participation in the liturgy will cultivate knowledge of the scriptural foundations of the Mass and Christ's real presence in the Blessed Sacrament. It will attend to the Eucharistic doctrines of the Church (including real presence and transubstantiation). This catechesis will offer a comprehensive initiation into the various parts of the Mass, enabling every man and woman to understand what is happening in the Eucharistic liturgy.[7] Catechesis will show how the Eucharistic mystery is echoed in the lives and writings of the saints, as well as in art and literature. All the sources of catechesis—including scripture, teaching of the magisterium, the liturgy itself, saints and martyrs, theology, Christian culture, and art—have a place in promoting knowledge of the faith.[8]

2. Integral Eucharistic catechesis must teach people to pray the Mass.

The *Directory for Catechesis* states that liturgical formation "educates the believer in the attitudes that the Church's celebrations require: joy for the festive quality of celebrations, a sense of community, attentive listening to the word of God, confident prayer, praise and thanksgiving, awareness of symbols and signs."[9] The *Directory* is dealing ultimately with dispositions or capacities that the believer brings to the Mass. Yes, praying the Mass in a reverent way—described in the previous chapter—is the best way to receive this catechesis. But if one treats Sunday as just another day, full of work to prepare for the week, it is unlikely that the faithful Mass-goer will be able to pray the Mass with joy. If we are unable to listen with attention, perhaps addicted to surfing the Web, we may not be able to listen to the Word of God. An integral Eucharistic catechesis, therefore, will teach people to pray the liturgy well through fostering dispositions of prayer.

3. Integral Eucharistic catechesis forms us for life in Christ.

Too often, our catechetical textbooks reduce this third task to ethics. How are we to live upright lives? But the *Directory* underlines the Christo-centric dimension of this task of catechesis:

> Catechesis has the task of making the heart of every Christian resound with the call to live a new life in keeping with the dignity of the children of God received in Baptism and with the life of the Risen One that is communicated through the sacraments. This task consists in showing that the response to the lofty vocation of holiness . . . is a filial way of life that is capable of bringing every situation back to the way of truth and happiness that is Christ.[10]

What is normally understood as the moral task of catechesis is to cultivate a deeper desire for holiness or total union with the person of Christ. Every dimension of my life is to be lived considering Jesus Christ, the One who gives himself to me in love upon the Eucharistic altar. My identity as a teacher, a husband, and a father is to be attuned to the sacrificial love that I learn from Jesus Christ. This task is really about the Eucharistic vocation of every man and woman to offer their bodies as a sacrifice of love back to the Father, through the Son, infused with the gift of the Holy Spirit.[11] Each Catholic is to learn the art of Eucharistic discernment, discovering the presence of Jesus Christ here and now.

4. Integral Eucharistic catechesis must initiate the Catholic into the art of prayer.

The capacity to recognize the presence of our Eucharistic Lord in our lives necessitates an education into contemplation: "Catechesis has the task of educating the believer for prayer and in prayer, developing the contemplative dimension of Christian experience."[12] Here, the *Directory* does not mean the kind of contemplation that was often spoken about by saints such as John of the Cross or Teresa of Avila—a mystical union with God that comes only as gift. Rather, a contemplative attitude is shaped by the one who prays both like and with Jesus. Contemplation is learning to take up the attitude that Jesus has before the Father. Prayer is not just something we do once a week at Mass. It is to permeate every aspect of our lives. Even as I am writing this book, I should be doing so in a prayerful manner. The catechetical setting should be a prayerful space—not a lecture hall, but a space where together we contemplate in praise, adoration, thanksgiving, and awe the mystery of divine love offered to us by Jesus Christ. In learning this contemplation, our whole lives become an extension of the Eucharistic mystery.

5. Integral Eucharistic catechesis fosters community life.

We are not saved all by ourselves. Rather, active participation in the Mass calls us into a spirituality of communion where we "see the light of the Trinity reflected in the face of one's brother . . . feeling through the profound unity of the mystical Body that he is part of oneself; sharing his joys and sufferings in order to perceive his desires; taking care of his needs; offering him a true and profound friendship."[13] This task of catechesis is a formation of every Christian into the Eucharistic communion of the Church. My parish is not full of strangers but is made up of those with whom I share the most intimate communion in Jesus Christ (whether, by the way, I like them or not). When I receive the Blessed Sacrament, our Lord's presence dwelling among us, I do so in communion with my neighbor. All of us together as the Church pilgrimaging through history have a responsibility to bring this Eucharistic communion into the hellish places of human history.

Notice that nearly everything in these various tasks relates even more to adulthood than to childhood. If our parishes are bereft of opportunities for adults to contemplate the Eucharistic mystery, we will never become a fully Eucharistic people in the parish. Our children will master the implicit curriculum that we are proposing to them—namely, religious formation is really for kids and, therefore, not that important. When you become an adult, you can move on to more serious things. The Eucharist is great for second graders, but what does it have to do with the rest of our lives?

- Think about catechesis in your parish across all ages and stages. Does catechesis in your parish attend to each of the five tasks laid out above?
- What do you wish you better understood about the Eucharist or the celebration of Mass?

A EUCHARISTIC CATECHESIS OF IDENTITY: MEMORY, UNDERSTANDING, AND DESIRE

Of course, now we reach a key pastoral problem. If adult Eucharistic catechesis—performed considering all the tasks of catechesis—is considered pivotal to fostering a Eucharistic culture, how should we conduct this catechesis? This is where most parishes go wrong. Parishes simply adapt what we do with children to adults. We get bigger chairs. Yes, we set them up in the parish hall rather than in the third-grade classroom. But we still adopt a classroom mentality to this education.

Let's be honest. This approach does not work in most places. We arrange for adult catechesis, but we only end up with a half-dozen adults gathering at 7:00 p.m. in the parish hall to hear about the Eucharist. Moms and dads, putting their kids to bed, never show up. Young adults cordon themselves off at Theology on Tap sessions. Many older folks cannot leave their homes in the evening. Yes, if you have a world-famous speaker come in (Bishop Barron–esque), you might fill the parish hall. But there are only so many world-famous speakers, they are often expensive, and they do not stick around after talking. Culture, remember, is about a worldview. No fly-by-night speaker can create a culture.

Ironically, retrieving an insight from catechesis from the early and medieval Church might be helpful to our problem. Namely, catechesis was related to the formation of a holistic sense of Christian identity that could not be accomplished in the classroom alone. Rather, the memory (closely linked to imagination), the understanding (or intellect), and the desire (or will) of the person receiving catechesis were cultivated in an integral manner. Let us explore the implications of this traditional insight for an integral catechesis today.

MEMORY, IMAGINATION, AND EXPERIENCE

If our primary experience of catechesis was before the Second Vatican Council, we might have a negative reaction to the word *memory*. We could think about our own catechesis as a matter of mere "memorizing" rather than understanding.

But, as the *Directory* underlines, memory is not reducible to memorization. The document states:

> Memory is an integral dimension of salvation history. The people of Israel are constantly urged to keep memory alive, not to forget the Lord's benefits. This is a matter of storing up in the heart the events that vouch for God's initiative, which at times are difficult to understand but are perceived as salvific events. . . . In its deepest sense, therefore, memory hearkens back to the primacy of grace; to the recognition of God's gifts and to gratitude for these; to live within a tradition without cutting its roots. Catechesis makes good use of the celebration or *memorial* of the great events of salvation history so as to help the believer feel part of this history.[14]

It is crucial to keep in mind that memory is not just a technique for storing information. It is linked to a personal appropriation of history—for our purposes here, *salvation* history. If I remember what God has accomplished, if it becomes part of me, then I too am part of that memory. And whenever I remember what the Father has accomplished through the Son, I experience anew a Eucharistic gratitude. What Jesus has done matters once again to me here and now. It matters because it is part of me.

This account of memory has its roots in the teachings of St. Augustine of Hippo. The fifth-century Doctor of the Church speaks about memory as a mansion or storehouse. Our senses take in so many things. Growing up in East Tennessee, there was the sweetest of smells that marked the arrival of summer for me. Even sitting in northern Indiana, far away from the foothills of the Smokies, I can experience anew that early summer sweetness in my memory. And when I am in Knoxville in June, when my nose takes in that most distinct of smells, I immediately experience once again what it's like to be a young boy hiking in the mountains. All the memories are at once retrieved. St. Augustine of Hippo, taking up these same themes, confesses about memory:

> Now I arrive in the fields and vast mansions of memory, where are treasured innumerable images brought in there from the objects of every conceivable kind perceived by the senses. There too are hidden away the modified images we produce when by our thinking we magnify or diminish or in any way alter the information our senses have reported. There too is everything else that has been consigned and stowed

> away. . . . Sojourning there I command something I
> want to present itself, and immediately certain things
> emerge, while others have to be pursued for some
> time and dug out from remote crannies. . . . The
> huge repository of the memory, with its secret and
> unimaginable caverns, welcomes and keeps all these
> things, to be recalled and brought out for use when
> needed.[15]

St. Augustine is highlighting that memory is closely linked to who we are, our very identities. What we have sensed, what is "written" upon memory, makes us who we are. All that I have experienced is a part of who I am.

Augustine is speaking about two things that we value in catechesis today. First, he is addressing experience. In Latin, the word for "experience" is *sentire*, where we get the word *sense*. To have an experience, therefore, is to undergo sensation. As I am writing this paragraph overlooking the St. Joseph River in South Bend on a beautiful summer day, my senses are experiencing the world around me. The remarkable aspect of this experience, of course, is that it becomes part of me. Later tonight, as I go to bed, I will be capable of recalling this experience. I will remember the color of the leaves reflecting on the water, the warmth of the sun, and the sound of the crickets around me.

This leads to the second dimension of experience addressed by St. Augustine. When your author remembers the experience of writing, he is engaged in an imaginative act. We often think of imagination as related purely to the fanciful. A child is imaginative if she thinks about a dragon chasing her through the neighborhood. But imagination is the capacity that we have as human beings to "remember" all that we have experienced. As I gaze upon the St. Joseph River, all the rivers I have canoed upon are brought before my interior gaze. In midwinter, I can think about every river I have ever swum in, almost feeling the refreshing water on my skin. You can see why Augustine might confess the wondrous power of memory.

Augustine is not interested in memory for its own sake. He wants to think about the formative power of memory in the Christian experience. Yes, I have canoed upon and have swum in dozens of rivers in my lifetime. This pales in comparison to my experience of the Eucharist. During my nearly forty years of life, I have attended thousands of Masses. I have prayed the Psalter in the Liturgy of the Hours. I have beheld and listened to hundreds of pieces of Eucharistic art and sacred music. This is all part of me, shaping my experience.

Remembering our experiences is always complicated. After all, I have attended many Masses. I have also been to countless Notre Dame football games, driven my car more than I care to think about, and told my children (almost every night) not to drink bath water. I have a lot of memories. The task of a Eucharistic catechesis for adults is to bring forth Eucharistic memories that enable us to fully become what we receive in the Eucharist, the Body of Christ for the life of the world.

How do we do this? First, as I addressed in the last chapter, we need beautiful Eucharistic liturgies—the kind of liturgies that stick in our memories. You can think about such reverent and beautiful liturgies as underlining what is memorable in the first place. They are kind of like a picture frame around an image, focusing our attention on what is before us. Do not look at the wall, but look at this Monet painting. Look beyond this beautiful liturgy to see the Lord.

But that is not enough. After all, the aesthete—someone who loves beauty for its own sake rather than as an occasion to know God—could also have a memory full of beautiful liturgies, but that does not make him love the Eucharist. We need to be intentional about filling our memories with all sorts of things related to the Eucharist, including theology and scripture. Whenever I receive the Eucharist at Mass, no matter the hymn, I remember the words of Psalm 34: "Taste and see that the LORD is good." If I did not know this psalm, its relationship with the Eucharist, then I might never think about it. But because I possess this memory, I can see more in the Blessed Sacrament than what I might initially behold. Yes, there is the Host before my eyes, so plain, so simple. But as I come forward to Communion, I am tasting and seeing the very source of all divine goodness. The words come to my mind, I recall them, and then my very experience of receiving the Eucharist is transformed.

Art is very important in the Eucharist. Art penetrates our senses. It becomes part of our memory. I can never attend Mass without thinking about the altarpiece I beheld at Ghent in Belgium. The image of the Lamb surrounded by all the saints, worshipping before the heavenly altar, always comes to mind when I receive the Blessed Sacrament. That experience of beholding a classic piece of art and my experience of going to Mass are linked in my memory. Every time I smell incense at Mass, when I behold the Blessed Sacrament on the altar, I see in my mind's eye (my memory) the Ghent altarpiece.

A Eucharistic catechesis will attend to memory by giving us a moment to behold. Beholding takes time. It is like when we read sacred scripture, and we simply rejoice initially in the words that we hear. We do not yet ask questions. But we wonder what our Lord means when he says that he is the bread of life in John 6. The more beautiful Eucharistic signs we behold—discernable in the scriptures, in art, music, literature, and poetry—the more we will be attuned to seeing what is happening in Mass. Our experience of Mass will be shaped by our memory and imagination, and vice versa.

UNDERSTANDING AND THE ART OF MEDITATION

If *memory* is a bitter word for many in catechesis, *understanding* is not much better. It recalls too often an understanding of catechesis as pure intellectual act. Church life becomes simply about those who have the academic credentials to earn it. Not a few apostolates today in the Church fall victim to this temptation, thinking that intellectual insight will fix everything.

This is not a proper understanding of understanding (sorry, I love word play). "Understanding" is the English translation of the Latin word *intellectus*. *Intellectus* refers to the human capacity to recognize the sense of something in what we behold. It relates to meaning.

Let me describe a moment of intellectual insight that will stretch our understanding of *intellectus*. When I travel, I call home. The first voice I often hear is my daughter's. The joy of calling home, though, is not just hearing the voice. This voice has a meaning. To listen to my daughter's voice, to hear the way that she calls me "Daddy," is *meaningful*. Her voice represents to me her being, the gift she is not only to her parents but to everyone who encounters her. When I hang up the phone, it's not the end of my meditation upon Maggie's voice. Traveling makes me *think* how important this creature is to my identity and to my life. In this whole process, I am engaged in an act of understanding, of meditation upon the gift of my daughter.

Understanding, then, is really an occasion of meditation. We take what we have sensed, what we remember, and we ask questions of it. We wonder about it anew. Maybe I hang up the phone and think to myself, "How can I love someone so much? How does this change the way that I think about love?"

Understanding in Eucharistic catechesis is not about mastery. It's about reclaiming wonder. The first way that we seek understanding of the Eucharist is by asking questions. These questions will not be purely academic. They will be personal— that is, involving our whole persons. How did my participation at Mass change my life? Why do I struggle so much with going to Mass? Do I live the Eucharistic love I receive in the Blessed Sacrament? All of these are acts of understanding.

Here, Eucharistic doctrine has a privileged place. We fail if we think about Eucharistic doctrine only as explanatory. Eucharistic doctrines are about *meaning*. The dogma of real presence offers us a hypothesis, a proposition to apply to our own lives. It says to us: The Lord dwells among us here and now. In my life, in my town (no matter how important), the Lord is there. He becomes present, and he wants me to become present to him, to adore him. Transubstantiation is the same. It's not about intellectuals treating the Eucharist as a philosophical puzzle. Jesus gives everything to me, and he now takes me into his way of marking time. What does my life mean if this ordinary bread and wine becomes Christ's Body and Blood? What does it mean that God gives himself fully to me under the signs of bread and wine? Am I willing to recognize in the Eucharist the ultimate gift that God is offering, the transformation of all creation?

You can see here that Eucharistic understanding or the *intellectus* is not something for Catholics who like to read Eucharistic tomes. Understanding is a concrete meditation on the meaning of the Eucharist for me and for all. I must ask questions of the Blessed Sacrament, to wonder anew before what is given to me. The Mass questions me, asking me to ponder its meaning for me here and now.

Let me give an example I have used in other writings on the Eucharist. What does it mean in the *Gloria* when I give praise, bless, adore, glorify, and give thanks to God? Doesn't this seem excessive? Inefficient? Praising and adoring—they basically are the same. But this thought misses out on something key. I praise and adore and bless and glorify because I am entering into the presence of God. It is not about efficiency. I must prepare myself for what I am to receive at Mass, the total presence of our Lord. As I ask questions about each part of the Mass, wondering what they mean, I'm really asking about the meaning of the Blessed Sacrament for my life. Do I glorify God in every dimension of my life? Do I approach the Blessed Sacrament sufficiently aware of the gift that I am receiving, a gift so tremendous that a single word for "praise" is insufficient for my preparation?

This approach to understanding is very closely linked to memory. After all, what we experience in our senses, what becomes part of us in our memory, often leads to new questions and insights about our common life in Christ. Over the last five years, I have taught a class at Notre Dame on the Eucharist and sacred art. I have studied altarpieces, chant, hymnody, architecture, poetry, literature, and sculpture. What I have contemplated has become part of my memory, leading me to approach the Mass anew and to ask new questions about the meaning of the Eucharist for me. The more that I experience and behold in wonder, the more questions I have about the meaning of the Eucharist in my life.

This approach to catechesis takes time. A catechesis that attends to both the memory and the understanding must give space for adults to encounter beauty, to wonder, to ask questions, and to dialogue and discern. Through cultivating this Eucharistic understanding, we become Eucharistic disciples.

Love and Desire

At the heart of all Eucharistic catechesis for children and adults alike is love. Again, the word *love* might not be received well by those engaged in catechesis. It could call to mind an approach to catechesis where doctrine is in short supply and the end of every lesson involves the creating of a craft project. In this approach, the only thing we need to know is that God loves us.

Of course, that's a misunderstanding of what we mean when we say that God loves us. In his own instruction of the North African catechist Deogratias, St. Augustine writes:

> What stronger reason could there be for the Lord's coming than that God intended to reveal his love among us and prove it with great force? For even when we were still his enemies Christ died for us. And he did this because *the object of commandment* (1 Tm 1:5) and *the fullness of the law is love* (Rom 13:10), his purpose being that we too should love one another, and that, just as *he laid down his life for us,* so too *should we lay down our life for the brothers.*[16]

For Augustine, love is God's great rhetorical strategy. Unable to get through to us in any other way, the Father sent his Son into the world. Despite humanity's rejection of God (as we see on the Cross), God kept loving us. He fulfilled the Law, wooing us to a deeper love not only of God but also of one another. *Love* in this case means total, self-giving friendship with God and neighbor alike.

When we say that God loves us, we are not thereby saying something trite, easily dismissed, or reducible to crafting projects for kindergarten catechesis. That God is love is the most radical thing we could believe. The source of everything, of all truth and goodness and beauty, loves us. Every dot and tittle of scripture, every liturgical rite, and every ecclesial teaching is about self-giving love.

The tragedy is that we do not always love God in return. Or we love God "sort of" or "kind of." Now, we may believe everything about Catholicism, even talk about it with friends, but the rest of our lives testifies against our love of God. We know what is good, we have studied it, but we struggle to love it.

Our habits have often made it difficult for us to love God with our whole heart, mind, and soul. Like most US citizens, I am addicted to my smart phone. An hour of the waking day does not pass by without a desire to look upon my phone. I did not learn this from a book or other media. I learned it because of the endless habit of touching and looking at my phone. I know that this practice keeps me away from reading books, which is part of my job. It makes it difficult for me to follow an argument to its end because I am often so distracted. I know what is good for me, but I struggle to live the truth that I know. Put down your smartphone, I know. But there I am again and again. Unlocking. Looking. Surfing.

The same goes with religious practice. Yes, I know that prayer is good for me. I know that God loves me, and therefore I should love God in return. I should set time aside to be with God. But I can't. I can't because I have grown into other habits. Rather than spend an hour before the Blessed Sacrament each week, I am open to doing literally anything else—for example, watching endless YouTube videos.

A Eucharistic catechesis for adults will take on an ascetical tone. In a chapter dedicated to words that no one likes, *asceticism* may take the cake. When we think of asceticism, a picture of a dour monk who never smiles, who is obsessed over every sin, may come to mind. But this is a misunderstanding of asceticism.

Asceticism is discipline. It is the response of a lover who wants to learn to love more.[17] If I cannot find time to pray, I could get up an hour earlier. I would sacrifice sleep for the sake of love. If I have grown accustomed to the gift of the Blessed Sacrament, no longer aware of the great gift that I am receiving in the Blessed Sacrament, I may try to spend thirty extra minutes before Sunday Mass alone with our Lord. If I ignore the presence of Christ in the poor, separating the reception of Jesus from the works of mercy, I may need not only to tithe but to dedicate an hour or more of the week to caring for the hungry and thirsty.

None of these practices, of course, is intended to get God to love me. God loved me first. God made the first move. But these practices create space for me to become a more perfect lover of God. They enable me to grow in holiness. Asceticism is ultimately about desire rather than punishment.

As we begin to practice our Eucharistic faith through Holy Hours, Benediction of the Blessed Sacrament, attending Mass more frequently, engaging in Eucharistic processions, and crossing ourselves as we pass by churches, we develop new habits. The new practices no longer hurt but become integral to our lives of faith. We are not earning God's grace, proving ourselves to Jesus. Jesus clearly does not want that. Rather, we are learning to become lovers of God. As the Eastern theologian Jean Corbon writes:

> Here is located the true fasting of those who willingly
> persevere in prayer: they sit at the table of hungry

sinners. Prayer then makes its own the desire of the Beloved Son, who came to share with others the paschal meal at which he gives himself. But who shall ever be capable of singing the joy of the Holy Spirit, the great Hallel of this mysterious banquet? For the more a heart consents to this kind of prayer, the more the Spirit unites himself with it in the kenosis of love.[18]

Corbon is describing the way that desire in prayer works. The more that we recognize our longing to be in union with Christ, to desire participation in the great Hallel (referring to the Jewish festival psalms) or festival of divine love, the more we share in the relationship that Jesus has with the Father. We recognize how empty we are. That is what the word *kenosis* means. It is a Greek word, referring to "self-emptying." We are empty not because we are not worthy but because our desire for God is so much that there is nothing we can possess that can quench our love.

A Eucharistic catechesis without the desire of love becomes a dry apologetics or an approach to religious formation in which the purpose of Catholic life is to lift ourselves up by the bootstraps of our practices and thereby prove ourselves worthy of divine love. A Eucharistic catechesis of love, however, means that every dimension of catechesis should be infused with desire, cultivating a love beyond all telling for the Eucharistic Lord.

- Having learned about the roles of memory, understanding, and desire, what insights have you had about an adult approach to catechesis? What implications can these ideas have in your parish or Catholic school?

EUCHARISTIC FORMATION IN SMALL GROUPS

Memory, understanding, and desire of love might be important for developing an integral approach to adult Eucharistic formation. But what would it look like to do such adult catechesis? Especially if we are not simply going to follow a classroom model?

Over the last fifty years, the Church has held up a model of adult education in small groups. These groups began in Latin American and were called *comunidades eclesiasles de base* or "base ecclesial communities." They read scripture together, reflecting on their lives in light of what was read. Everyone, no matter how poor, was invited to engage in this dialogical process.

In the United States, this small-group approach has taken over many of our parishes, especially around Bible studies. Groups like Evangelical Catholic, FOCUS, and RENEW International focus on small group conversations around sacred scripture. The *Directory for Catechesis* highlights its importance for parish life throughout the world:

> The Christian community is the primary agent of catechesis. For this reason, catechetical pedagogy

must make every effort to convey the importance of the community as a fundamental space for personal growth. The communitarian model is also visible in the dynamic of the group, the concrete place in which to live out "new relationships brought by Jesus Christ" that can "become a genuine experience of fraternity." Paying attention to group relationships has a pedagogical significance: it develops the sense of belonging to the Church and assists growth in the faith.[19]

Group catechesis is not just a technique for evangelization; it is constitutive of an integral religious formation. We learn to be Catholic, to become a Eucharistic people together.

Can we take the insights raised by base ecclesial communities and small-group outreach in evangelization movements and apply them to an integral Eucharistic formation? Yes! After all, the same reflection that takes place in small-group Bible studies can take place around the Mass, contemplating the lives of Eucharistic saints, or in a series of sessions dedicated to discussing the relationship between Catholic social teaching and the Eucharist. The McGrath Institute for Church Life's Notre Dame Center for Liturgy has resources on our website that do all of this. But in case you want to create your own, each of these resources moves through three steps.

Step 1: The beginning of the small-group conversation involves turning one's attention to some dimension of the Eucharist worth beholding.

It might be an image of an altarpiece, a specific architectural feature of the Church, sacred scripture, a text or ritual practice of the Mass, a poem, or a piece of sacred music. In the group, we create space and time to behold together the beautiful object. Being together in silent prayer helps create a Eucharistic community, those who have learned to pray with one another. Further, our common Eucharistic memory is enriched in this process.

Step 2: Wonder, as you remember, is not just about staring at some object. It means asking questions of what we have beheld.

If we have just read St. Thomas Aquinas' hymn on the Eucharist, we begin to ask questions. The questions can be anything, especially if we want to cultivate the freedom of the person. Questions can be about the meaning of words, the history of what we have beheld, why it is important to me, how it makes me think differently about attending Mass or my life, and so on. A facilitator creates questions for guidance, but the facilitator is not the master of the common inquiry.

Step 3: At the end of this conversation, there is a return to silent prayer.

We are invited to think about what we have learned, how it has shaped us. We imagine what practices we will perform over the next week considering what we have contemplated in this session. We may even mutually pledge to participate in a concrete practice together as a group. Morning Mass, a work of Eucharistic mercy (addressed in the chapter 5), or a common Holy Hour. Spending time with the Beloved is the emphasis of the last stage, returning to an act of love that deepens our desire for union with Christ.

One small note about these communities. They need not be so formally organized that they become impossible for a pastoral staff to manage. Such communities could be cultivated in neighborhoods rather than at 7:00 p.m. at the parish (probably, better for families with young children anyway). They can be integrated into already existing parish communities such as moms' and dads' groups. Adaptations can be made so that families can engage in this reflection together. Youth and young-adult ministries can also take up these common reflections on the Eucharistic mystery.

It is important as the *Directory for Catechesis* highlights that none of these groups forget that it is the Sunday assembly that is the community of all communities. Small groups cannot be a replacement for the flesh and blood encounter we have with other Catholics on a Sunday morning, who each come to adore the Eucharistic Lord. For it is there that a Eucharistic spiritual of communion is best fostered in the parish.

- What did you learn about catechesis in this chapter? How might an integral Eucharistic formation benefit your parish in becoming Eucharistic People?
- What other small-group discussion topics might you be interested in relative to an integral, adult Eucharistic catechesis? Please email us at ndcl@nd.edu with these ideas!

4.

A EUCHARISTIC POPULAR CATHOLICISM

A theme throughout this book has been the Eucharistic vocation or calling of the Catholic. The celebration of the Mass is not just something that we do on Sunday mornings; every Catholic is called to consecrate the world to Christ through their lives. It is this vocation to publicly witness to the Lordship of Jesus that is the objective of cultivating a Eucharistic culture in the parish.

Thus far in this book, we have attended to the *ad intra* or intramural dimensions of fostering this Eucharistic culture. We become a Eucharistic people through enculturated reverence in the liturgy and an integral Eucharistic formation of the People of God. But there is an *ad extra* or extramural dimension of this formation too. A Eucharistic culture must extend outside the walls of the church into the world. Leaving nothing behind from our encounter with Jesus in the Blessed Sacrament, our sacrifice of praise we offer at Mass, and our contemplation of this mystery of love, we are called into our families, jobs, and neighborhoods to make present Christ's Eucharistic love for the life of the world.

The remaining two chapters will complete our portrait of a Eucharistic culture by attending to popular Catholicism and Eucharistic solidarity. Everything that we have reflected on thus far is not left behind. Becoming Eucharistic people necessitates that we take up all four dimensions of a Eucharistic culture.

A EUCHARISTIC POPULAR CATHOLICISM

The term *popular Catholicism* might be initially confusing. For many English readers, *popular* is linked to fame. A person who is popular has a lot of people who like them. Popularity relates to that which is fashionable, and Catholicism is not trendy.

This is not the meaning of the word *popular* exclusively, either in English or in Spanish. *Popular* means "of the people." Popular or public Catholicism is therefore an approach to Catholicism that is of the people. It is a lived Catholicism, which moves outside the doors of the parish into families and neighborhoods. The Catholic theologian Roberto S. Goizueta writes about popular Catholicism:

> Whether in the *Posadas*, the Christmas reenactment of Joseph and Mary's search for lodging; or the *mañanitas* sung to Our Lady of Guadalupe on the morning of her feast day; or the *Via Crucis* of Good Friday; or the annual pilgrimage to the holy chapel at Chimayo, New Mexico; or the celebrations on the Day of the Dead; or the family prayers offered on the home altar, Latinas and Latinos experience the palpable, loving

> presence of a God who walks with us in the daily
> rhythm of life in family, neighborhood, and com-
> munity. . . . The Catholicism of Latinas and Latinos
> . . . tends to be a Catholicism rooted, first, not in the
> parish but in the home, in the neighborhood.[1]

Goizueta is highlighting the way that Catholicism is lived in
families and neighborhoods and not exclusively in the Eucharistic liturgy. Processions, the singing of hymns, and domestic
devotions make up a popular Catholicism that is celebrated by
the baptized faithful in the world. This Catholicism of the people
remains alive and well among Latina and Latino Catholics and in
places like Poland. But in much of Europe and the United States,
popular Catholicism has been forgotten.

What happened? This is a complex question, outside the
scope of this book. But let me acknowledge one cause of the
decline of popular Catholicism. In the twentieth century, liturgical scholars overemphasized a distinction between liturgy and
devotional life. Afraid that Catholics did not understand the
importance of the Eucharistic liturgy, much Church teaching
underlined that the liturgy of the Church forms the basis of the
devotional life, not the other way around. Yes, devotions such
as the Stations of the Cross, the Rosary, lighting candles before
statues, and pilgrimages have a place. But the public prayer of
the Church in the formal liturgical rites are where we should
place our focus.

Ironically, this almost myopic focus on liturgy has led to a
privatization of Catholic life. Catholics know how to go to Mass
on Sunday for an hour. But that is about it. Many Catholics do

not know how to pray the Rosary at home. Without the official liturgy of the Church, they have no life of prayer. The COVID-19 pandemic proved this. Most parishes responded to social distancing, not by encouraging the practice of a domestic, popular Catholicism, but instead by livestreaming Masses.

Consequently, without a popular or lived Catholicism, the liturgies in our parishes suffer. It turns out that while a theological distinction between liturgical rites and popular piety is possible (the former involves a minister of the Church, the latter does not), the same distinction is not viable relative to human experience. After all, I am but a single human being. The person who goes to Mass on Sundays is the same person who participates in *Posadas*, who goes to Stations of the Cross during Lent, who lights candles on graves on All Souls' Day, and who yearly remembers the baptismal anniversaries of our children. Baptized into Christ, I exercise my baptismal priesthood in the holy sacrifice of the Mass and by engaging in a popular Catholicism in my neighborhood.

As Goizueta points out, it is often those places where popular Catholicism is alive and well that parish liturgical life is also flourishing.[2] This is because in such places Christianity has not been overly spiritualized, deformed into a series of philosophical principles instead of a living encounter with the incarnate God. As Goizueta writes, "The greatest threat to faith is precisely that represented by a rationalist or spiritualist Christianity that preaches a God without a world; a Christ without a face, without a body, without wounds; a cross without a corpus."[3]

If a parish is to become a Eucharistic people, then we must recultivate a popular Catholicism, one that does not separate the liturgical life and devotional life of the person. We must admit that many US parishes have severed the link between the two, ignoring the importance of lived Catholic practice. Latin American Catholic cultures—present in the United States from the beginning—provide an opportunity to restore a popular and therefore Eucharistic Catholicism.

- Is popular Catholicism—as defined by Goizueta—integral to the identity of your parish. If so, how do you know? If not, why?

RESTORING A EUCHARISTIC AND DEVOTIONAL CATHOLICISM

How do we restore what has been lost in many US parishes? Simply, we need to reclaim the devotions that have been important to Catholics for so many generations.

These devotions are themselves part of the Eucharistic faith of the Church rather than separate from it. As we have seen throughout this book, everything that is authentically human can find a place in the Mass. When we pray the Rosary with our families, we are engaging in a moment of remembering the mysteries of Christ's life that we bring into the Eucharistic liturgy. A woman who lights a candle before a statue in a quiet church is engaging in a Eucharistic act of intercession. Her faith and hope in a God who listens to the cries of the poor is made present in the sanctuary. A Mexican parish in a city that goes from home to home, enacting the Holy Family's search for a space to sleep, makes present the Eucharistic mystery of Christmas. Love has come to dwell among us, even if we do not recognize it.

Eucharistic devotions are pivotal to reconnecting the chain of devotional practice in our parishes. The 40 Hour Eucharistic devotions, involving the entire parish, allow the Eucharist to permeate all space and time. Holy Hours transform our hearts to love the Eucharist more. I remember when I was an undergraduate and did a Holy Hour every Tuesday morning at 2:00 a.m. I woke up in the middle of the night, bundling up to endure a ten-minute walk in the snow to pray before the Blessed Sacrament in Fischer Hall chapel. I was not always entirely cognizant of my prayer. I sometimes fell asleep. But this devotional practice allowed the Eucharist to integrate into every hour of my day, becoming so important to me that I would be willing to wake up in the middle of the night to visit our Lord.

Further, these Eucharistic devotions also allow for more affective dimensions of piety than we sometimes experience at Mass. Benediction of the Blessed Sacrament, with hymns that allow us to raise our hearts and souls to Christ, only increases our capacity to pray at Mass.

Eucharistic Processions

Eucharistic processions are also important to restoring a popular, embodied Catholicism. Now, let me be clear. Processing through neighborhoods with the Blessed Sacrament will not suddenly lead to Catholics streaming to Mass. This is the kind of magical thinking that often infects the Church around evangelization.

Still, these processions are fundamentally popular and therefore integral to the faith of the People of God. In the medieval Church, the Feast of Corpus Christi (the Body and Blood of Christ) was marked by Eucharistic processions through city streets. Such processions made manifest a key dimension of Eucharistic faith. The Mass was not only about the reception of Jesus Christ but about the Eucharistic solidarity of the whole neighborhood.[4] Everything in the city could be transformed by the Eucharistic presence of our Lord. Not everyone was a devout believer, or a regular communicant, but through these Eucharistic processions they found a way to participate in the mystery of divine love that cannot be limited to the celebration of Mass in the parish or cathedral church.

Eucharistic processions were celebrated in the medieval Church at other occasions, too, including Rogation and Ember Days. Rogation and Ember Days were times of prayer and fasting preceding both planting and harvest. The spring Rogation Days (celebrated before the Ascension) included walking the boundaries of the parish with the Blessed Sacrament, as well as the celebration of litanies and other blessings along the way.[5] These processions manifested something about the Eucharistic identity of the parish. Mass was not a private event, just for those gathered in the church. The Eucharist had implications for everyone in the geographic boundaries of the parish—the love of God bound everyone together. Further, all that the people have received, including the fruits of field and forest, are gifts from our Eucharistic Lord.

The Eucharistic Family

Popular Catholicism, as Goizueta noted, holds up the importance of domestic religious practice. In Latina and Latino Catholicism, it is often the faith of an *abuela* (grandmother) or *madre* (mother) that captures the imagination of children. One learns a powerful Eucharistic faith in the context of the home, discovering the way that the presence of Jesus and his mother, Mary, changes everything.

Retrieving a Eucharistic popular Catholicism necessitates, therefore, an emphasis on the family as the domestic church. When I say that the family is the domestic church, I want to emphasize three caveats.

1. To call the family the domestic church is not merely a helpful metaphor.

Rather, insofar as the family is a manifestation of divine communion in the world, a place where the love of Christ and the Church becomes present, the family is really and truly a domestic church.[6] By its nature, the family is therefore Eucharistic, inviting every person to experience the love of Christ in the imperfect communion of husband, wife, and (God-willing) child(ren). The family, when gathered in prayer and blessing, or when remembering the feasts of the Church year, is an authentic manifestation of Christ's love for the world.

2. **Because of the Eucharistic identity of the family as a space of communion in the world, we must avoid a romanticized account of the family.**[7]

Yes, the family has a vocation to guard love. Moms and dads are integral to this task, even if the domestic church is not reducible to what is often called the nuclear family. But a popular Catholicism recognizes that family life is complicated. It is not some angelic mode of existence, where children are always perfect, and moms and dads get everything right all the time. Otherwise, nearly every family I have encountered (especially my own) would be excluded.

3. **The family is a domestic church in relationship to the concrete celebration of the Eucharistic mystery in the parish.**

This means that the family must learn to become what is received in the Eucharistic mystery, a communion of love that exists for the life of the world.[8] All that we have said about an integral Eucharistic formation in chapter 3 is therefore important for the family. The memory, understanding, and desire of the family must be suffused with the Eucharist.

Still, there are three ways that the family contributes to a restoration of a popular Catholicism that is essential for a Eucharistic culture.

1. **The family is a place of Eucharistic memory.**

It is within the family that the liturgical feasts of the Church become part of daily life.[9] In my family, we commonly remember the lives of the saints as part of our day-to-day experience. Sundays are savored as the family spends time together in holy leisure. We make pink cakes for *Gaudete* and *Laetare* Sundays, and we fast together on Ash Wednesday and Good Friday by eating tomato soup and a bit of bread for dinner. The mystery of Christ's life is no longer an abstraction but lived in the flesh-and-blood ways that are normal to families.

2. Families pray together.

It is important in our family that we have created a separate space for prayer, full of icons and candles for the sake of our common worship. Yes, we go to Sunday Mass. Sometimes, we go on weekdays too. But what happens in Mass does not stay there. We raise our voices to God each night as we sing hymns and psalms of praise. We mark liturgical time in these prayers, changing what we say and sing as the seasons of the Church year move along. We bless one another.

3. We practice in daily family life all the dispositions necessary for Eucharistic worship of God.

We forgive one another transgressions both large and small. Each day around the dinner table we share what we are grateful for. We practice hospitality, welcoming friends, neighbors, and my students into our home. Not only do we cultivate these dispositions, but we talk about why they are important to us. Parents are the first catechists of their children, not because they are necessarily explaining every doctrine to their children. Rather, they are the first catechists because they explain why the mystery of Christ's life is so important to the culture of the family.

THE EUCHARISTIC VOCATION AT WORK

A large portion of our lives consists of work. And yet, how often do we speak about work at the parish? A public Catholicism, which is popular in form, demands that we consider the Eucharistic quality of our labor. This call to think about the Eucharistic dimension of our day-to-day labor is not new. The great Jesuit liturgical theologian Josef Jungmann wrote:

> If the Church comes to life in the participants in the actively celebrated liturgy, then a new relationship to the surrounding world comes into being; a new relationship to the material world itself, to the world of trades and professions. For it is real men of flesh and blood who are caught up in the process of the liturgy. It is their voices, their goings and comings which have become part of the sacred action. It is the bread from the work-a-day world which is carried to the altar. It is the work of the tradesman's hand which appears in the sacred furnishings and decorations, in the building which encloses everything. It is the every-day world which is drawn into the sacred action, joined with the sacrifice which Christ presents with his Church assembled here.[10]

The Christian possesses a Eucharistic vocation, which moves outside the parish walls into one's life at work. The teacher consecrates existence back to the Father through the act of education. The nurse does the same through caring for those who are sick. Such moments of consecration bring us back to the altar, where we stand in the presence of Jesus Christ, offering him our loving service for the life of the world.

What happened to Catholics that we have forgotten this? And how can we reclaim it? Simply, we need to give men and women in our parish occasions to reflect on the sacred quality of the work they perform. We are talking about vocation not as something abstract but as the flesh-and-blood way that we live out our identities as baptized priests of Jesus Christ in the world. An annual Eucharistic retreat in the parish (an outline is found in the online resources), focused on the theme of work, is one way of retrieving the Eucharistic quality of labor in our parishes. Further, such a retreat would form men and women to see their identity as Catholics not as something private, only for themselves, but as something given for the flourishing of their neighbors. Renewing a Eucharistic vision of labor already brings us to the theme of the next chapter, cultivating Eucharistic solidarity in the parish.

CONCLUSION

Everything that is authentically human can find a place in the Eucharist. And that means a popular Catholicism, celebrated not just within the walls of the parish church, is integral to cultivating a Eucharistic people. Devotional life, Eucharistic processions, the domestic church, and a Eucharistic vision of vocation are part and parcel of restoring a popular Catholicism to US Catholic life. And as we will see in the final chapter, parish renewal is linked closely to cultivating a Eucharistic solidarity with the whole neighborhood.

- How might popular Catholicism, as laid out in this chapter, serve as a salve against a private Catholicism focused only on the individual?
- Think about devotions that you learned as a child or adult. How are they Eucharistic in the way defined by this book?
- Family and work are both defined by the Eucharist. How? Does your parish treat families and workers as Eucharistic? If you don't (or you could do better), what ideas did this chapter generate for you? Are there ways that you could use the resources available online for cultivating a Eucharistic popular Catholicism in your parish setting?
- Visit https://eucharisticrevival.org/about/#resources to get outlines of potential ways of worshiping the Eucharist outside of Mass including Eucharistic Processions and adoration of the Blessed Sacrament.

5.

A CULTURE OF EUCHARISTIC SOLIDARITY

Some years ago, I presented a paper on the Eucharistic orientation of Catholic social teaching at a conference. I thought that the argument of the essay was uncontroversial. The Eucharistic sacrifice of Jesus Christ, the gift of divine love, is integral to the Church's vocation to transform the public sphere into a space of communion. Catholic social teaching and the Eucharist are intrinsically connected. Like most academic papers (from unknown scholars of little import), it was attended by no more than a handful of people, including a young man who had committed himself to social justice. He raised his hand, befuddled. What did the Mass—in the end—have to do with his public advocacy of those on the margins? To justice? How could spending an hour each week, praying with the Church, really help him solve the problem of poverty?

The young man's question could be asked in almost every parish in the United States. Yes, most of us recognize that the Church has a certain responsibility in the public sphere. We should raise our voices against assaults on the human dignity of the unborn, the migrant, and the prisoner. But what does this political advocacy have to do with the Eucharist? Isn't such advocacy an addendum for the interested?

As I have written elsewhere, because of a severing of Catholic social doctrine and the Eucharist, the social teaching of the Church remains unknown and unappropriated by most Catholics.[1] This is bad news, harming the capacity of the Church to offer a public witness to the world of the gift of divine love. Many of our parishes, as I noted at the beginning of this book, are polarized on the social questions of our day. We are inspired more by the policies of Democrats and Republicans than by our commitment to the Eucharistic vocation of the Church, the beautiful responsibility to transform every crack and crevice of the world into a space of divine love.

The Church and the world suffer because of this severing, unable to give full witness to the marvelous possibilities given through the presence of Jesus Christ in every parish church. We must relearn the art of a Eucharistic solidarity, recognizing that the gift of receiving our Lord in the Blessed Sacrament comes along with a renewed commitment to love of neighbor. A Eucharistic culture, therefore, must cultivate a Eucharistic solidarity among the People of God. This Eucharistic solidarity will be marked by Eucharistic coherence, Eucharistic works of mercy, and a prophetic witness to a politics of communion in the public sphere.

WHAT IS EUCHARISTIC SOLIDARITY?

In 2017, I visited the city of Gdańsk in the northern part of Poland. It was in this city that the Solidarity movement in Poland began. Solidarity (*Solidarność*) in Poland was a social movement that witnessed to the dignity of the worker against the communism imposed on Poland by the Russians. This movement relied upon nonviolent protest, even when the state reacted violently against the protestors. And because Poland was impossibly Catholic—contrary to the Russia's desire—religious practice was integral to the movement. Spending two hours in a museum dedicated to the movement, I was moved by videos of men in the shipyard confessing their sins to priests, receiving the Blessed Sacrament, and continuing to uphold the dignity of the worker. This public witness was at least partially responsible for the collapse of communism in Poland.

Karol Wojtyła (now known as St. John Paul II) was privy to this movement, at least from afar. He had been elected pope in 1978. And yet, he had been formed by a long social tradition of solidarity that was integral to Poland. Under his papacy, the theme of solidarity was given prominence in Catholic social teaching. In his 1987 document *Sollicitudo Rei Socialis (The Social Concern)*, the saintly pontiff upheld the importance of solidarity for the entire human family. Solidarity, as I said earlier, is not just a vague feeling. It is not a fancy way to say, "I feel you, bro!" Rather, solidarity is the recognition that my neighbor is a person. As humans we share something fundamentally in common with one another—the category of personhood. Because we share our identity as persons in common, your suffering means something to my life. I cannot ignore it.

As St. John Paul II wrote, solidarity "is not a feeling of vague compassion or shallow distress at the misfortunes of so many people, both near and far. On the contrary, it is a firm and persevering determination to commit oneself to the common good; that is to say to the good of all and of each individual, because we are all really responsible for all."[2] Because we share the human condition with one another, your good and my good are inextricably linked. To take an example that might be controversial, I might wear a mask during a pandemic not because I am afraid of dying myself. Instead, I wear the mask for your good. I do not want you to get sick and to die. I might even advocate in the public sphere for a public mask mandate (again controversial) because I believe that I have a public responsibility to the good of the whole community of men and women.

Importantly, for St. John Paul II, solidarity is accessible to reason. But like all dimensions of Catholic social teaching, it takes on a richer dimension when bearing in mind the Gospel. He writes:

> In the light of faith, solidarity seeks to go beyond itself, to take on the specifically Christian dimension of total gratuity, forgiveness and reconciliation. One's neighbor is then not only a human being with his or her own rights and a fundamental equality with everyone else, but becomes the living image of God the Father, redeemed by the blood of Jesus Christ

> and placed under the permanent action of the Holy
> Spirit.[3]

My life and your life is a gift. Yes, I can think about my obligation to consider your rights. You are a person, after all, possessing such rights. But as a Catholic, I move beyond the limits of reason alone toward divine revelation. You are a son and daughter of the living God, someone created because God loves you. Solidarity in a Christian key, therefore, is marked by gift, forgiveness, and friendship.

A Christian approach to solidarity was taken up by Pope Benedict XVI in his encyclical *Deus Caritas Est (God Is Love)*. Importantly, the pope emeritus connects solidarity with the Eucharist. He writes:

> Faith, worship and ethos are interwoven as a single
> reality which takes shape in our encounter with God's
> agape. Here the usual contraposition between wor-
> ship and ethics simply falls apart. "Worship" itself,
> Eucharistic communion, includes the reality both of
> being loved and of loving others in turn. A Eucharist
> which does not pass over into the concrete practice
> of love is intrinsically fragmented. Conversely, as we
> shall have to consider in greater detail below, the
> "commandment" of love is only possible because it is
> more than a requirement. Love can be "commanded"
> because it has first been given.[4]

Read this passage again. Even though the word *solidarity* is not mentioned, Pope Benedict is describing a Eucharistic solidarity. In

Christianity, because God is love, there is no separation between faith in God, worship of God, and the kind of people we become because God first loved us. Liturgy and ethics are both exercises of worship. The gift of receiving Jesus Christ in the Blessed Sacrament, therefore, calls us to an exercise of solidarity. We are to love others. And if we do not, the Eucharistic mystery of the Church is fragmented or fractured. The commands of holy scripture—to love God and neighbor—are therefore not laws in the strict sense. Rather, they become responses to the gift first given. In the Eucharist, I receive total love. So I seek to give it away. The flourishing of my neighbor is part of this gift.

Pope Benedict's account of the Eucharist and ethics is what I mean by Eucharistic solidarity. It is the recognition that my neighbor—a person like me—is a gift. He or she is owed a return gift of love, not only because he or she possesses rights. For the active Catholic, this return gift of love is part of the Eucharistic mystery. I receive the gift of love in the Eucharist not because I deserve it. I serve my neighbor not to get something out of it. I do these because all of us exist in an economy of gift. God loves us; therefore, we love one another. Every time I receive the Blessed Sacrament—the gift beyond all gifts—I commit myself to my neighbor's flourishing. The gift I have received from Jesus, through Jesus, and with Jesus is to be passed on.

The Eucharistic mystery, therefore, is not just the benefit of Catholics. It is the entire human family—every person who suffers from indignity—who is to benefit from what happens upon the altar. Here I am speaking not just about the consequence of mission. Yes, *Mass* means "sent." But mission does not begin only at the end of Mass. In our reception of Jesus Christ in the Blessed Sacrament, we are already committing ourselves to love our neighbors in our daily lives.

Eucharistic Coherence

Of course, we know that we do not always love our neighbors. We do not immediately become what we receive in the Eucharist—that is, the total self-giving love of Christ given for the life of the world. But this weakness does not mean that we should never receive the Eucharist at Mass. Pope Francis reminds us of this in his apostolic exhortation *Evangelii Gaudium (The Joy of the Gospel)*: "The Eucharist, although it is the fullness of sacramental life, is not a prize for the perfect but a powerful medicine and nourishment for the weak."[5] If we only received the Eucharist when we felt as if we had earned it, proved ourselves worthy of grace, then we would miss the whole point. The Eucharist would become a prize for the perfect instead of a medicine for the weak.

At the same time, in calling the Blessed Sacrament a medicine, Pope Francis presents the quality of the Eucharist as a gift. We cannot interpret the Holy Father's words as saying that everyone should receive the Eucharist every time without second thought. After all, I might say, God is merciful, and therefore God does not care if I am incoherent in my Eucharistic reception, if I am cheating on my spouse or intentionally underpaying those who work for me. But to receive the gift of divine love, I need to see the Eucharist as a medicine intended to heal me of my sickness. I cannot schlep toward the altar, receive Jesus, and then continue sinning in the exact same way. No, as St. Paul reminds us in his First Letter to the Corinthians, I would be receiving to my own condemnation.

If we are to cultivate a Eucharistic people committed to Eucharistic solidarity, we must first attend to Eucharistic coherence. Eucharistic coherence is not just for Catholic politicians.[6] We are all called to Eucharistic coherence, to receive the gift of love given in the Blessed Sacrament and thereby to offer that same gift of love to our neighbors.

In this sense, Eucharistic coherence is an opportunity for the whole Church—including the pope, bishops, priests, deacons, and the baptized faithful—to discern our commitment to Eucharistic solidarity. Take the sexual abuse crises that have embroiled the Roman Catholic Church, especially the most recent revelation of a clerical culture that rewards silence. Eucharistic coherency requires us to leave behind that clerical culture and to care for the victim. Dioceses that have laid off lay employees, often not following Catholic social teaching relative to the dignity of the worker, are Eucharistically incoherent.

Here the Church must recognize the corporate quality of sin. We ought to confess our sins in common through regular celebration of the Sacrament of Penance. We, as the Body of Christ in the world, have not always lived up to our identity. Dioceses, parishes, and religious communities have failed.

And, of course, I as an individual have also failed. St. John Paul II always mentioned sacramental Reconciliation in close connection with the Eucharist. There is a reason for this. To receive the Blessed Sacrament means that I seek to love as Jesus Christ did. If I cheat on my spouse, am angry at my students, or treat a coworker with contempt, I am Eucharistically incoherent. At Mass, I confess that incoherence often. I confess my sinfulness, telling all of you that I am unworthy to receive Jesus in the Blessed Sacrament. But I must also reflect regularly on my life and receive the forgiveness of Jesus in Confession before approaching the Blessed Sacrament. And in receiving that forgiveness, I am reconciled to you, my neighbor in the Church. We belong to one another. My sins, even if you never know about them, hurt you.

So it is Eucharistically incoherent if I do not know who you are. Our parishes are full of men and women who have no idea who their neighbor is. COVID-19 reminded us of this. How many of us had no idea who was alone, without anyone to deliver them groceries? Who in our parishes were suffering from unimaginable loneliness? To receive the Blessed Sacrament means that I must be in solidarity with you in all your concreteness. Your good is my good. If I do not know you, then I am Eucharistically incoherent.

None of this should make us feel totally inadequate, which falls back into the trap of confusing the Eucharist as a prize for the perfect. Since the Blessed Sacrament is a medicine of mercy, I do need to confess that I am not worthy of that gift. Who is? And the more I recognize my unworthiness, the more I will reshape my life into a coherent offering of love bestowed to my neighbors.

- Think about your life. Are you Eucharistically coherent? Where do you need to change?
- Ask the same questions, but this time about your parish or diocese.
- Look at the suggested service for a parish-based Reconciliation available online. How does the act of penance restore us to practice Eucharistic solidarity?

Eucharistic Works of Mercy

Maybe you have heard something like this before: the real work of justice is not charity but changing structures. To a certain extent, this is true. After all, it is better that my neighbor is no longer hungry or a prisoner than that I feed or visit him. St. Augustine himself often said this in his sermons, noting that in heaven there will be no hunger or prison. There we will have perfect charity and justice alike. But we are not yet in heaven. Meanwhile, the hungry and the prisoner need both food and companionship.

There is something problematic about the claim that justice and charity are at odds. Simply, we need love. We are embodied creatures. No matter what laws are passed, I still need human companionship. I still need food. The concrete, embodied service of my neighbor is necessary for me because my neighbor and I are both human. And Jesus Christ, after all, became human. He became a neighbor to us, healing the sick and feeding the hungry in a flesh-and-blood way.

Traditionally, the Church has upheld this flesh-and-blood service as works of mercy. The works of mercy are fourteen-fold. There are the corporal works of mercy, which include feeding the hungry, giving water to the thirsty, clothing the naked, sheltering the homeless, visiting the sick, ransoming the captive, and burying the dead. The spiritual works of mercy are instructing the ignorant, counseling the doubtful, admonishing the sinner, bearing patiently with those who offend, forgiving offenses, comforting the afflicting, and praying for the living and the dead. Because the corporal works of mercy involve the body more directly, we might forget how physical each of the spiritual works of mercy are too. After all, teaching and counseling are embodied activities. We are giving ourselves to the other, in a flesh-and-blood way. Anyone who has ever served as a catechist to sixth-grade boys knows that the love that is bestowed very much so involves being present to the other.

Each of these works of mercy, in fact, is inspired by the Eucharistic gift of love. If we cook dinner for the homeless one evening, for example, we are not doing anything remarkable, or at least not anything that we should reward ourselves for. We are simply returning the gift of love that we have received. The same goes for teaching undergraduates about the deficits of hookup culture.[7] Such an act of education is simply a return gift of love to a primordial gift that is bestowed in the Eucharist.

In this sense, if we want to practice Eucharistic solidarity, we should begin to live out the works of mercy. Parishes that focus on Eucharistic Adoration, but do not possess a St. Vincent de Paul Society or do not have enough catechists, need to ask questions.

Have we understood what is given in the Eucharist? Do we grasp that such a wondrous gift must also be given away?

- Look over the resources online dedicated to the works of mercy. What makes each work of mercy Eucharistic?
- What could your parish do to better cultivate these Eucharistic works of mercy as acts of solidarity?

Politics of Communion

At times, this book has been an exercise in rescuing words that we hate from all the terrible connotations that such words possess. As we conclude our chapter on solidarity, we perform one last exercise of retrieval. This time, we turn to the word *politics*.

Politics, of course, has a bad rap in the Church. For lots of folks in the United States, they do not want their churches to engage in politics.[8] Church and state are separate. What we really want at church is spiritual nourishment, not another version of CNN or Fox News.

On the other hand, we know how politicized the Church can be. It has often been said that many American Catholics more closely identify with their political party than with their Church. So not a few Democrats are happy to speak about the dignity of labor and bracket out the unborn. Republicans purport themselves as radically pro-life, except for the migrants on the border.

And yet, the Church is called to engage with the *polis*. The root of the word *political* is, after all, *polis* or "city." We are called to engage with the public square, to create spaces of love in what is at times a loveless or hellish world. In this sense, the Church is the most political of all entities out there. We are called to transfigure the city of men and women into the city of God.

The theologian William T. Cavanaugh has something to offer us in our consideration of this problem. Americans are suspicious of politics in religion. And yet, we also are highly politicized. Maybe what we need is a Eucharistic sense of politics. Cavanaugh writes:

> The Eucharist is not simply a promise of future bliss outside of historical time. In the biblical and patristic witness we find the Eucharist as an earthly practice of peace and reconciliation. Paul reprimands the Corinthians for continuing divisions between rich and poor, and suggests that some of them are sick and dying *now* because they have partaken of the Eucharist without first reconciling these divisions (1 Cor. 11:17–32). Where peace is lacking, the Eucharist appears as . . . a sign of judgement requiring that people reconcile before a true Eucharist can take place.[9]

The Church celebrates the Eucharist not as Republicans or Democrats but as the People of God. The Church seeks to bring all men and women into the Eucharistic communion of the Church. This communion is marked by a peace so radical that we can barely imagine it. The sacrifice of Christ should end the desire for violence against our neighbors because Jesus has declared the nullity of this violence through his Death and Resurrection.

Love alone wins. Love descends into the darkest spaces of human relationships, transforming them—transforming us.

Let us be frank. We have not figured this out, especially as citizens of the United States. We are so attached to our own liberty that at times we forget that our lives are given to us. We have been given all things as gift. Abortion, racism, hatred of the migrant, the death penalty—these are assaults upon human dignity and therefore upon the gift of existence. They are evidence that we have not yet taken seriously enough the Eucharistic politics of the Church, where the only gift we can offer back is the sacrifice of Jesus, a presence of love that changes everything.

Cardinal Bernardin's consistent ethic of life or Pope Francis's teachings warning against a throwaway culture are part of a Eucharistic politics. Every human being was created to offer the sacrifice of love unto the end, which the Church conducts in the Eucharist. This call to Eucharistic solidarity and not just individual spirituality is hard for many of our parishes to hear. We are immersed in the politics of hatred and blame endemic in US society today. We can do better. But the way forward is through the Blessed Sacrament, with a common discernment of the ways that the Church can witness in the public sphere to a Eucharistic politics of communion.

How can we do this in the parish, without making everyone hate each other? The path forward is learning to have real dialogue on questions that matter to the *polis* and the parish alike. Are we willing to dialogue over difficult issues? To commit ourselves to witnessing to the dignity of our neighbor, in an act of Eucharistic solidarity, no matter the cost?

But the real task is to return to the altar, to discover anew something we confess at Mass: that all—every man and every woman—are called to the supper of the Lamb.

- Be honest. Is your parish polarized over politics? How?
- How might the Eucharist allow you to move forward if you are polarized? How might the Eucharist help you to uphold the dignity of each and every human life?
- Gather a group of parishioners to take our course on Catholic Social Teaching and the Eucharist. What did you learn as you took this course about Eucharistic solidarity and politics alike?

CONCLUSION

To receive the Blessed Sacrament is to commit ourselves to Eucharistic solidarity. We are to love our neighbors with the same Love that we have received in the Blessed Sacrament. This is hard work. But it is why we keep returning to Mass, receiving our sacrificial Lord so that we can consecrate every dimension of the cosmos to Christ. This is what Eucharistic solidarity, in the end, is—a love-transformed cosmos.

CONCLUSION: A PLACE WHERE HEARTS ARE CONTINUALLY AFLAME

Early in this book, we noted that disaffiliation is a big concern after COVID-19. Those who did not go to Mass during the pandemic might not come back. And that means we might see declining participation in the Church in coming years.

The solution to this problem is not as easy as it is often presented. We hear people say that if we just change Church teachings on *x*, *y*, or *z*, then everyone will come back. Or if we teach doctrines *x*, *y*, or *z*, then everything will be fixed. It is not so simple. Many people find it hard to commit to any institution. We are increasingly aware of hypocrisy, and we demand that our institutions are congruent with their deepest identity.

This book has proposed that as Catholics our deepest identity is the Eucharist. We are a Eucharistic people, those who have received love and thereby are called to give it away. That is our hopeful mission as a Church, a Eucharistic Church who assembles around the real presence of her Lord. Only then will we live as Eucharistic People, possessing a culture infused with the self-giving love of Jesus Christ poured out for the life of the world.

But we must learn to become what we have received. So this book has invited you and your parish into a process. It has not bestowed all answers (but many of our online resources will help with a common act of discernment). The hope is that, through reading this book, you will be able to initiate a Eucharistic revival in your corner of the cosmos. One that leads men and women, who are otherwise suspicious of ecclesial belonging, to take more than a second look. Perhaps they will come, see, and stay with us. For they might recognize, in worshipping with us in our parishes, that their hearts were burning all along. And, just maybe, our Church is where hearts are continually aflame with a love beyond all telling. At least, that's what Jesus promised to us.

NOTES

PREFACE

1. John Aberth, *The Black Death: A New History of the Great Mortality in Europe, 1347–1500* (New York: Oxford University Press, 2021), 103–21.

2. Pew Research Center, "In U.S., Decline of Christianity Continues at Rapid Pace," *Pew Forum*, October 7, 2019, https://www.pewforum.org/2019/10/17/in-u-s-decline-of-christianity-continues-at-rapid-pace/. Accessed August 21, 2021.

3. USCCB, "The Mystery of the Eucharist in the Life of the Church," https://www.usccb.org/resources/The%20Mystery%20of%20the%20Eucharist%20in%20the%20Life%20of%20the%20Church.pdf. Accessed November 24, 2021.

4. Timothy P. O'Malley, *Real Presence: What Does It Mean and Why Does It Matter?* (Notre Dame, IN: Ave Maria Press, 2021), 10.

5. Louis Bouyer, *The Church of God: Body of Christ and Temple of the Holy Spirit*, trans. Charles Underhill Quinn (San Francisco: Ignatius Press, 2011), 295.

6. The book is an expansion upon an earlier article of the author. See "The Difference Between Liturgical Naïveté and a Eucharistic Culture of Affiliation," *Church Life Journal*, June 15, 2021, https://churchlifejournal.nd.edu/articles/a-eucharistic-culture-of-affiliation/. Accessed August 21, 2021.

1. WHAT IS EUCHARISTIC CULTURE?

1. Timothy P. O'Malley, *Divine Blessing: Liturgical Formation in the RCIA* (Collegeville, MN: Liturgical Press, 2019), 15–56.

2. Second Vatican Council, *Gaudium et Spes (Pastoral Constitution on the Church in the Modern World)*, December 7, 1965, no. 53, https://www.vatican.va/archive/hist_councils/ii_vatican_council/documents/vat-ii_const_19651207_gaudium-et-spes_en.html.

3. Michael Paul Gallagher, SJ, *Clashing Symbols: An Introduction to Faith and Culture*, 2nd ed. (London: Darton, Longman & Todd, 2003), 25–26.

4. Pope Benedict XVI, *Sacramentum Caritatis (The Sacrament of Charity)*, February 22, 2007, no. 2, emphasis original, https://www.vatican.va/content/benedict-xvi/en/apost_exhortations/documents/hf_ben-xvi_exh_20070222_sacramentum-caritatis.html.

5. Benedict XVI, *Sacramentum Caritatis (The Sacrament of Charity)*, no. 10, emphasis original.

6. Benedict XVI, *Sacramentum Caritatis (The Sacrament of Charity)*, no. 11.

7. Benedict XVI, *Sacramentum Caritatis (The Sacrament of Charity)*, no. 52.

8. Pontifical Council for the Promotion of the New Evangelization, *Directory for Catechesis* (Washington, DC: USCCB, 2020), nos. 79–89.

9. Timothy P. O'Malley, "Slow Catechesis: Liturgy, Popular Piety, and Beauty in the Directory for Catechesis," in *Together Along the Way: Conversations Inspired by the Directory for Catechesis*, ed.

Hosffman Ospino and Theresa O'Keefe (New York: Crossroad, 2021), 79–97.

10. Benedict XVI, *Sacramentum Caritatis (The Sacrament of Charity)*, no. 71.

11. Benedict XVI, *Sacramentum Caritatis (The Sacrament of Charity)*, no. 83.

2. A CULTURE OF EUCHARISTIC REVERENCE

1. Romano Guardini, *The Spirit of the Liturgy*, trans. Ada Lane (New York: Crossroad, 1998), 82–83.

2. Pope Francis, *Evangelii Gaudium (The Joy of the Gospel)*, November 24, 2013, no. 164, https://www.vatican.va/content/francesco/en/apost_exhortations/documents/papa-francesco_esortazione-ap_20131124_evangelii-gaudium.html.

3. See Uwe Michael Lang, *Turning Toward the Lord* (San Francisco: Ignatius Press, 2009).

3. A CULTURE OF INTEGRAL EUCHARISTIC FORMATION

1. Timothy P. O'Malley, "My 8-Year-Old Son Has Taught Me—a Sacramental Theologian—How to Love the Sacraments Again," *America Magazine*, April 1, 2021, https://www.americamagazine.org/faith/2021/04/01/sacraments-initiation-theology-eucharist-restored-order-240270. Accessed August 16, 2021.

2. Pontifical Council for the Promotion of the New Evangelization, *Directory for Catechesis* (Washington, DC: USCCB, 2020), no. 75.

3. See Sofia Cavalletti, *The Religious Potential of the Child: Experiencing Scripture and Liturgy with Young Children* (Chicago: Liturgy Training Publications, 2021).

4. See Jane E. Regan, *Toward an Adult Church: A Vision of Faith Formation* (Chicago: Loyola Press, 2002); Jane E. Regan, *Where Two or Three Are Gathered: Transforming the Parish through Communities of Practice* (New York: Paulist Press, 2016).

5. *Directory for Catechesis*, 260.

6. Romano Guardini, "A Letter from Romano Guardini," *Herder Correspondence* (August 1964): 239.

7. See Timothy P. O'Malley, *Bored Again Catholic: How the Mass Could Save Your Life* (Huntington, IN: Our Sunday Visitor, 2017).

8. *Directory for Catechesis*, no. 90–109.

9. *Directory for Catechesis*, no. 82.

10. *Directory for Catechesis,* no. 83.

11. Timothy P. O'Malley, *Liturgy and the New Evangelization: Practicing the Art of Self-Giving Love* (Collegeville, MN: Liturgical Press, 2013), 76–107.

12. *Directory for Catechesis*, no. 86.

13. *Directory for Catechesis*, no. 88.

14. *Directory for Catechesis*, no. 201, emphasis original.

15. Augustine of Hippo, *The Confessions*, trans. Maria Boulding (Hyde Park, NY: New City Press), X.8.12–13.

16. Augustine of Hippo, *Instructing Beginners in Faith*, trans. Raymond Canning (Hyde Park, NY: New City Press, 2006), I.4.7, emphasis original.

17. See David Fagerberg, *On Liturgical Asceticism* (Washington, DC: Catholic University of America Press, 2013).

18. Jean Corbon, *The Wellspring of Worship*, trans. Matthew J. O'Connell (San Francisco: Ignatius Press, 2005), 215.

19. *Directory for Catechesis*, no. 218.

4. A EUCHARISTIC POPULAR CATHOLICISM

1. Roberto S. Goizueta, *Christ Our Companion: Toward a Theological Aesthetics of Liberation* (Maryknoll, NY: Orbis Books, 2009), 50.

2. Goizueta, *Christ Our Companion*, 71.

3. Goizueta, *Christ Our Companion*, 82.

4. Miri Rubin, *Corpus Christi: The Eucharist in Late Medieval Culture* (New York: Cambridge University Press, 1991), 243–70.

5. Eamon Duffy, *The Stripping of the Altars: Traditional Religion in England c. 1400–1580* (New Haven, CT: Yale University Press, 1992), 136–39.

6. Timothy P. O'Malley, "The Embodied Mystery of the Family: A Liturgical Theology of the Domestic Church," *Listening: Journal of Communication Ethics, Religion, and Culture Winter* (2018): 48–58.

7. Timothy P. O'Malley, "De-Romanticizing the Domestic Church: The Liturgical-Sacramental Vocation of the Christian Family," in *Renewing Catholic Family Life: Experts Explore New Directions in Family Spirituality and Family Ministry*, ed. Gregory K. Popcak (Huntington, IN: OSV Institute, 2020), 29–46.

8. Timothy P. O'Malley, "The Liturgical-Sacramental Identity of the Domestic Church: Combatting Domestic Romanticism by Means of the Liturgical Act," *Antiphon* 24.1 (2020): 1–18.

9. Katherine E. Harmon, *There Were Also Many Women There: Lay Women in the Liturgical Movement in the United States 1926–59* (Collegeville, MN: Liturgical Press, 2012), 242–325.

10. Josef Jungmann, *Pastoral Liturgy* (Notre Dame, IN: Ave Maria Press, 2014), 344.

5. A CULTURE OF EUCHARISTIC SOLIDARITY

1. Timothy P. O'Malley, "The Agnostic Reception of Catholic Social Teaching," *Church Life Journal*, December 7, 2020, https://churchlifejournal.nd.edu/articles/the-agnostic-reception-of-social-encyclicals/. Retrieved on August 21, 2021.

2. Pope John Paul II, *Sollicitudo Rei Socialis (The Social Concern)*, December 30, 1987, no. 38, https://www.vatican.va/content/john-paul-ii/en/encyclicals/documents/hf_jp-ii_enc_30121987_sollicitu-do-rei-socialis.html.

3. Pope John Paul II, *Sollicitudo Rei Socialis (The Social Concern)*, no. 40.

4. Pope Benedict XVI, *Deus Caritas Est (God Is Love)*, December 25, 2005, no. 14, https://www.vatican.va/content/benedict-xvi/en/encyclicals/documents/hf_ben-xvi_enc_20051225_deus-caritas-est.html.

5. Pope Francis, *Evangelii Gaudium (The Joy of the Gospel)*, November 24, 2013, no. 47, https://www.vatican.va/content/fran-cesco/en/apost_exhortations/documents/papa-francesco_esortazi-one-ap_20131124_evangelii-gaudium.html.

6. Timothy P. O'Malley, "What's at Stake in the Debates Swirling around Eucharistic Coherence?," *Church Life Jour-nal*, June 29, 2021, https://churchlifejournal.nd.edu/articles/

what-is-at-stake-in-eucharistic-coherence/. Accessed August 21, 2021.

7. See Timothy P. O'Malley, *Off the Hook: God, Love, Dating, and Marriage in a Hookup World* (Notre Dame, IN: Ave Maria Press, 2018).

8. See David E. Campbell, Geoffrey C. Layman, and John C. Green, *Secular Surge: A New Fault Line in American Politics* (New York: Cambridge University Press, 2020).

9. William T. Cavanaugh, *Theopolitical Imagination: Discovering the Liturgy as a Political Act in an Age of Global Consumerism* (New York: Bloomsbury, 2002), 51–52.

Timothy P. O'Malley is a Catholic theologian, author, and teacher. He also serves in the McGrath Institute for Church Life at the University of Notre Dame as the director of education and academic director of the Notre Dame Center for Liturgy. O'Malley is an executive member of the Eucharistic Revival and a theological consultant for Laity, Marriage, Family Life, and Youth with the United States Conference of Catholic Bishops.

He also serves on the mission committee of the board of trustees at the University of the Incarnate Word in San Antonio, Texas, and as president of the Society for Catholic Liturgy.

O'Malley earned his bachelor's degree in theology and philosophy and his master's degree in liturgical studies from Notre Dame. He earned a doctorate in theology and education at Boston College.

He is the author of seven books, including *Real Presence* and the award-winning *Off the Hook*. His articles have appeared in publications such as *America* magazine, *Religion News Service*, *Angelus* magazine, and *Our Sunday Visitor*.

The McGrath Institute for Church Life was founded as the Center for Pastoral and Social Ministry by the late Notre Dame President Fr. Theodore Hesburgh, CSC, in 1976. The McGrath Institute partners with Catholic dioceses, parishes, and schools to provide theological education and formation to address pressing pastoral problems. The Institute connects the Catholic intellectual life to the life of the Church to form faithful Catholic leaders for service to the Church and the world. The McGrathInstitute strives to be the preeminent source of creative Catholic content and programming for the new evangelization.

Bishop Andrew H. Cozzens serves the Diocese of Crookston in Minnesota.

MORE IN THE
ENGAGING CATHOLICISM
SERIES

Books in the Engaging Catholicism series from
the McGrath Institute for Church Life at the University of Notre
Dame help readers discover the beauty and truth
of the Catholic faith through a concise exploration of the
Church's most important but often difficult-to-grasp doctrines
as well as crucial pastoral and spiritual practices.

Perfect for seekers and new Catholics, clergy and catechetical
leaders, and everyone in between the series expands
the McGrath Institute's mission to connect the Catholic
intellectual life at Notre Dame to the pastoral life
of the Church and the spiritual needs of her people.